SMALL BUSINESS IS BIG BUSINESS

YOUR FOCUS DETERMINES THE ULTIMATE SIZE OF YOUR BUSINESS.

JIMMY MUHINDA

SMALL BUSINESS IS BIG BUSINESS

Your focus determines the ultimate size of your business

Jimmy Muhinda
Agri-Move Limited
Kampala - Uganda
Tel: +256 (0) 772563048 | +256 (0) 702662840
©Jimmy Muhinda 2018.

For feedback and inquiries:
jmhnda@yahoo.com

ISBN- 978-9970-9933-0-7

FOREWORD

Get ready to go on an adventurous journey with this book. Regardless of where you find yourself right now in business or your career, I am sure a dream of being the next big popular brand or conglomerate has ever come to your mind. Every big business/brand or conglomerate we see today started as a small business. It all began with doing the right things in their order and timing.

Nobody is born immunised against entrepreneurial lows and highs but I found this book to be a vaccination against killer diseases in business. Jimmy took his time to reflect and in a detailed way show how it works; from the initial business set up to the epitome of massive scale up and sustainability, the book gives game changing nuggets that transform a small idea to a large business.

The goal of every entrepreneur is to grow, but unfortunately many fail after years and months of struggling. This failure is always caused by giving up when things aren't working well and agree with me 95% of the time things aren't working because of ignoring important concepts that would generate success. Jimmy takes you deep into those concepts in a way that is easy to adapt and get your business going from scratch to an eight figure revenue and massive impact. The concepts in the book are so catching and I highly recommend it as a must read for visionaries.

Nicholas K. Quest
Serial Entrepreneur, Consultant, Author and Trainer
Founder and Leader NBK-Premier Solutions,
Legacy Pearls Africa Ltd

DEDICATION

To my children, Comfort and Prosper, the two most precious gems in my life. One has been my comfort since coming into my life and the other has joined us at a time prosperity is beckoning us. This book has been a giant win against procrastination. May all of us have comfort in prosperity.

ACKNOWLEDGEMENTS

My illustrious mother, Ms. Jane.K.Mbabazi, who never stops supporting me in my life journey. She has been there for me whenever I needed her. I can never thank you enough for pushing me to get out of my comfort zone. She has never denied me anything in life and always wants what is best for me. I could not have asked for a better mother

My madam, Allen, who has been a rock since she came into my life. Thanks for being patient with me during this stressful time of writing and publishing this book. Thanks for taking good care of the home in my absence and allowing me to bring this new baby to the world. More good things are coming your way.

Friends who have persistently demanded that I put what I regularly share into a book for posterity. Your prayers have been answered. I have finally done it. Enjoy the fruits of your constant plodding. Thanks for believing in me way before I gathered the courage to write this book.

I sincerely appreciate a few friends who offered to do initial proofreading and who gave me feedback as I was writing this book. Joseph Nsenga, Jolly Nakibirango, Sarah Kisakye and Martha Nakakande occupy a special place in my heart. Your positive feedback turned this book into a better version. May your selflessness be richly rewarded.

Nicholas Katushabe turned into my accountability partner ever since I let it out that I intended to write a book. He regularly asked about the progress of fulfilling that promise. Thank you for keeping me focused on fulfilling what I started. He has unreservedly taken me through all the stages of writing and publishing a book. He read through my manuscript and agreed to write a foreword for the book. What could I have done without you. GOD BLESS YOU.

CONTENTS

INTRODUCTION

If you have a small business mind, you will stay small.

Often times, it is assumed that for one to be in business, one must be running a very big enterprise that operates on a huge capital base. This has discouraged people with limited capital from investing their money. They keep hoping that when money accumulates, they would then join business. Those with limited capital in their businesses have also failed to run business according to best practices and use such businesses to support their personal and family expenses. They draw money from these businesses at any time of their urging.

While growing up, I recall that nearly every child dreamt of becoming either of the big six; doctor, engineer, lawyer, architect, accountant or pilot. This is not about to change very soon because professionals are considered more employable. A few children dreamt of becoming business people and even fewer parents considered this route for them. The focus then —as is now— was studying very hard to make it to university to become a professional and be employed somewhere. The questions all of us should be asking are: "Are employers from planet Mars?" "How do they manage to put up businesses that employ graduates?"

Businesses have, for long, been considered an arena for the uneducated/less educated lot in the society. This perception has partly been informed by how badly the business proprietors and their employees handle customers and their complaints. Business people are widely described as shrewd and crafty because of their pursuit for profits. Even when we work for crafty business people, we would want the world to know that we do not make the decisions but are merely employees.

It is worse when an educated person is found doing business that is considered beneath their status. After all those many years in school, the societal perception is that such a person would be found in a big office or doing an extraordinarily large scale business. Being involved in what others consider as small business for survival is nothing to write home about.

Probably, the resentment towards doing small business is because most people we saw while growing up still do what they did then. We have become adults yet nothing seems to have changed in these people's lives apart from aging. They have not even moved a step away from the position/ place they used to operate from. They are either content with themselves or have an intense fear of venturing out and away from their usual place of operation.

With the ever increasing population and number of graduates, the competition for available job opportunities is getting harsher by the day. Students are graduating at a very fast rate compared to the number of new opportunities made available.

Our children ought to be informed that the biggest percentage of the working population is in what we term as small businesses. Small businesses are the engine on which countries are run because they employ the largest number of people compared to governments. Bigger businesses are going in for automation of their processes to reduce their wage bills hence more employees are bound to find themselves unemployed.

We need to undertake case studies of our forefathers and how they managed to amass wealth. Most of them started small and progressively accumulated unmatched wealth.

Though uneducated, the focused ones pushed all their children through school, own or owned large chunks of land, farms and others ventured into real estate.

Small businesses tend to offer services at more affordable prices which attracts a bigger part of society; the low income earners. They are easy to manage and replicate elsewhere. Their costs of operation are very manageable hence profitability is guaranteed. Productivity too is very commendable. Smaller areas are utilized to produce a lot of products. A case in point is urban farming and its productivity in comparison with the productivity of people still stuck in artisanal farming practices.

What we must emphasize to our children is the fact that every big company they see started as an insignificant entity in the community. The proprietors invested a lot of time, effort and money to put it where it is currently. The proprietors had big dreams and set out to realize them one step at a time. These children too can set targets and realize their dreams to become the next big thing of their generation.

Any business is as small as the proprietor looks at it and keeps it. If the proprietor decides to grow it bigger, it surely grows. And even without directly engaging oneself in the daily operations of the business, one can still supervise others to generate money from these businesses we call small businesses. Nothing limits us from starting several of such businesses apart from our capability to manage people and processes. Start and manage one successfully and you are on your way to growing bigger faster.

This book therefore sets out to encourage you to take those baby steps towards presenting something worthwhile to the world. Within each one of us is a potential we are yet to fully utilize. Fully utilizing our potential will result in more inventions and innovations, employment opportunities and more money in circulation.

It further tackles those personal behaviours and characters that affect the businesses we work for and with. The biggest hindrance to advancement in our professional and career paths is ourselves and our reaction to opportunities before us. Compare your behaviour and performance to those doing better in life. In most cases, these people have made deliberate choices about what they do and they put in extra effort in whatever they do. May this book jolt you into being a proactive participant in adding value to the enterprises you work for and as well help you be a better version of your current self.

Point(s) for action

Chapter One

BUSINESS DIFFERENTIATION

WHAT IS BUSINESS?

Business is what you make it to be.

According to the Oxford Advanced Learner's Dictionary, business is the activity of making, buying, selling or supplying goods or services for money. Business is the activity of making one's living or making money by producing or buying and selling goods and services. It is any activity or enterprise entered into for profit.

It is an organization where people work together. In a business, people work to make and sell products or services. Other people buy the products and services. A business can earn a profit for the products and services it offers. The word business comes from the word busy, and means doing things.

Anyone running a business must focus on achieving, maintaining and sustaining growth and profitability. They must maximize their output/sales yet minimize operational costs. A serious business is devoid of unnecessary wastage or leakages as a lot of effort is put in ensuring production but most importantly productivity. Work that is done must not only be effective but efficient as well. A serious business person must at all times ensure there is value for money and other resources invested in any kind of business.

Business is any activity carried out with an aim of making profit. If whatever you are doing does not bring in a profit, it ceases to be a business. Most of us unfortunately take businesses as hobbies. We put up "investments" with no intention of scaling up operations that would result in more profits. We pride ourselves in owning unique ventures but rarely provide required inputs to sustain them economically and profitably.

There are several businesses we ignore simply because they are either too basic or too complicated for us. These perceptions are some of the reasons why we never generate as much money as we would have. We avoid what is simple and can easily be scaled up or what we deem complicated yet hard to copy by every Tom, Dick and Harry only to settle for what makes us comfortable.

Any business we do should give us maximum satisfaction that everything is being done to provide unique services to customers who experience a memorable personal touch from us. Define that good feeling your customers must experience whenever they visit you and /or your premises and go ahead to ensure all your employees understand and provide it always.

The more customers feel pampered, appreciated and well catered for, the more they will be inclined to spend their money on your services. A satisfied customer shall always return to places where he/she derives maximum satisfaction. Make satisfying your customers your number one and only job in all interactions with them.

Anything we touch can be turned into a business. Around you is someone who is earning from something you could easily take for granted. Once you start generating profits from it, set higher sales targets and you will make more money hence profits. The amount of profits generated from any transaction will determine how fast and how far you will go in building a lasting business. Focus all your attention on finding ways of increasing sales and you will have a business for yourself worth being proud about.

Despising certain kinds of work has made most of us unproductive and/or underproductive. We feel certain kinds of work are fit for a particular grade of people. Not even the fat balance sheets of people who transact in those kinds of businesses can convince us to try them out.

The day you learn that what matters after a day's work or after a year is what investments you have made is the day you will follow the money. You do not have to personally engage in what you have no passion for. Smart people take lessons and research about what businesses generate adequate profits and mobilize the necessary resources to dive into them. Ask several questions about the business and get answers from people doing the business or those that deal with them.

When people realize you do not know the nitty gritties of a business, they will want to take advantage and cheat you. Never stop learning from those already in the same field and never totally delegate your supervisory functions. Supervising what goes on helps you understand the business better. Keep out of direct operations but maintain an overseer's presence in your business. Your visible presence is a much required check for any member who would want to utilize gaps to do what is not beneficial to the business.

Avoid transacting business solely over the phone or on records compiled for you. Anyone given too much freedom to transact on your behalf will tell you or compile records of what they want you to know. The only way to crosscheck what you are being told or shown is to physically go on the ground and talk to various members of staff.

WHAT IS SMALL BUSINESS?

Small is relative. Let your small business be a springboard for phenomenal impact.

A small business is any company that employs less than 500 employees or that falls beneath an industry-specific annual receipts cap. While this makes for quite a broad pool of organizations, most small businesses are significantly smaller than this, employing no more than a few dozen employees at most.

According to Uganda Investment Authority, a small business is an enterprise that employs 5-50 employees with total assets between Uganda shillings ten million to a hundred million.

According to the World Bank ranking, a small enterprise is one that employs 5-50 employees and has total assets or total annual sales of US dollars a hundred thousand to three million.

Many small businesses start as sole proprietorships or partnerships. Their owner(s) have total control over the business and their long/continued absence leads to the collapse of these enterprises. Sole proprietors or partners pay income taxes for business profit on their personal income tax returns and are legally liable for business debts.

Small businesses have limited access to financing. They largely receive financing from personal savings of owners, insignificant business loans from some banks, gifts, loans from friends and family members.

They are high risk to lend to because their success and survival largely depend on the continued good health, availability and competence of the owner or partners. Small businesses focus on a niche market. Their survival depends on perfectly identifying this niche market and satisfying its demands. They might be able to survive by selling a single product or service in a very specific market. Because of limited resources, they dread venturing into wider markets which would stretch their capacity to deliver.

In most, if not all, small businesses, one employee will be required to fulfil tasks of multiple employees. Because proprietors must minimize costs to survive, they hire fewer employees than is ideal. The pressure to excel in performance has to be borne by this skeleton staff.

Small businesses are, often times, qualified to be big businesses by our standards. Very few people employ that number of employees and neither do they have assets or sales turnover near what is talked about in the definitions explained above. The ones we dotingly call our small businesses are actually micro businesses by every standard.

If the small businesses, as defined, are out of our reach, let us focus on starting micro-businesses. These require fewer resources to start up and do not require too much supervision. We should strive to gain experience at this low level before launching out to start bigger enterprises that necessitate a lot of money and attendant resources. This level should actually be utilized to pick lessons because the money injected in most of them is not so much as to shock someone when lost in mistakes.

Once we do exceptionally well at the micro-business level, we are ready for the big league. Perfecting the principles will be easy as we deal with bigger numbers in terms of people and other resources.

WHAT IS BIG BUSINESS?

Big is defined by area of coverage, quality and quantity of output.

Big business is business that has specialized in providing services to as many people as possible wherever they are. Deliberate efforts are made to produce good quality products in adequate quantities and get them to every customer who needs them. They operate beyond one location and are focused on growing into other locations.

Big businesses offer more products and services to a wider variety of consumers. They branch into new markets and regularly offer new products and services to increase sales and hire more employees. Their survival is hinged on continued research and development into new innovations and making these easily accessible and available to the market.

Big businesses usually pay taxes separately from the owners. They have outgrown the vice of fusing business with personal accounts. They have understood that business money is different from personal money.

Owners do not directly manage the business but appoint an executive committee to do so. Owners agree upon the targets to achieve and hire competent people to coordinate all activities towards realizing these targets.

Big businesses attract financing from banks, investors and from venture capital firms.

They easily attract this financing because they are able to show past, current and future performance and trends backed by authentic data. They can also raise capital by selling shares of stock to the public or selling corporate bonds.

Big businesses are listened to by any government because they contribute a lot to the economy in terms of tax revenues and providing employment to the country's citizens. Any policies that are found to adversely affect these businesses are rescinded as soon as it is found out.

Big businesses have been designed to transcend generations and everything possible is done to continuously align any activities towards the overall goal. All employees share in the vision and mission of the enterprise and are required to work towards achieving set goals at all times. Big business thrives on setting up and strengthening of systems. Roles are clearly spelt out for everyone. Staff is hired for specific tasks and supervised to do them satisfactorily. Because employees will try all possible ways to break into any system you set up, regularly evaluate all systems.

In big business, the owners focus most of their attention on strategy and get less involved in routine operations. Routine activities do not give anyone ample and uninterrupted time to think strategically for a business.

These businesses attract a lot of incentives for them to operate anywhere they show an interest of establishing themselves. When set up, there is a ripple effect in the community around them.

They create employment for multitudes of community members and buy a lot of produce and products from these communities thereby enabling them to earn decent incomes. Infrastructure is also set up or improved to ease business for them and the community.

They master the art of marketing and enter several markets with their products. In pursuit of a sustainability program, they tend to engage the local community to mobilize necessary raw materials to enable them produce more. This triggers increased production in the surrounding community.

Big businesses carry out corporate social responsibility projects within the communities around them. In appreciation of their support, they set aside a portion of their revenues to improve the living conditions of the community members.

ARE YOU IN BUSINESS OR SIMPLY BUSYNESS?

Don't be a busy body. Be a productive body.

We all wake up daily with an intention of keeping ourselves working at something that should have an intrinsic value attached to it. For those employees who expect to be paid a salary at the end of every month, their input rarely is commensurate to the pay they get. They get to do as little as possible yet expect to be paid a full salary in addition to bonuses and other allowances. They will be busy at anything and everything apart from fulfilling their obligations at work. Some business owners allow this state of affairs to go on under their watch either because they themselves are guilty of the same indiscipline or they lack the guts to tell off such employees. Each and every employee must be busy doing what either brings in revenue or ensuring that the enterprises they work for do not make losses due to negligence during the stipulated time of work.

If business owners allow employees to behave like kids, they will have themselves to blame. Kids have no idle time but most of what they do in the time they have does not bring monetary returns to it yet they will be exhausted at the end of the day. Your employees should not be exhausted from sitting around, chatting, making and answering to personal phone calls and counting down the hours to departure time. Every employee must mean business by fulfilling their obligations without excuses. Turn the busyness of your employees into business by ensuring they account for the time they spend at the workplace.

Does your business pay you and cater for its own costs of operations?

We start businesses to be able to get profits as we serve customers, pay ourselves decent salaries and cater for costs of operations. At the beginning, you might not be able to generate adequate sales to pay you decently and still cover the other costs of operations. You must be able to have a backup plan to enable you survive during this period and also fund the business operations.

If you do not know the breakeven point of your business, you will never know when your business will start making profits. A breakeven point in business is that point at which the sales generated exactly cover the costs of operations (Total sales=Total costs).After the breakeven point, the extra sales enable the business to make profits. Depending on your type of business, you must know when it will start generating profits so that you mobilize adequate resources to enable you operate smoothly till that time.

Many people are still struggling to fund their businesses even after a long time. They complain that they get no money from them and have to get it from elsewhere to keep these businesses running. If your business does not pay you adequately and cover its costs of operations, even after a long period of time, you need to go back to the drawing board. Determine what the breakeven point of your business is and what amount of sales will enable you to start making profits. If it is hard for you to determine, then engage a consultant to help you come up with these figures.

You need to develop a budget that highlights how much money is needed to take you through the first six months of setting up a business. Mobilize this money in advance or at least be sure of where you will get it to fund the first six months. During this time, you need to focus on setting up systems and mobilizing necessary resources to strengthen your business.

Lacking money to pay short term bills will immensely affect the morale of employees and the proprietors. Although expenses must be kept at the minimum in the beginning, they must cover the basic needs of your workforce. If their basic needs are catered for, they can easily be convinced to hold on as working conditions are improved.

Point(s) for action

 SMALL BUSINESS IS BIG BUSINESS

Chapter Two

GROWING BUSINESSES

WHAT IS A GROWING BUSINESS?

We only grow by moving ahead in a deliberate fashion.

A growing business is akin to a growing child. A child goes through several growth phases that follow each other immediately. Every single step different from what the child has been used to is celebrated by parents. There is a lot of anxiety amongst parents wondering whether their child will progress from one stage to another within the anticipated timeframe. Parents are always on the lookout for those tell-tale signs that the child is growing well. God created within us the monitoring ability that should come naturally in whatever it is that we do.

A growing business therefore should show signs of moving from one step to the next. There must be a progressive change in the sales, customers, variety of adequate stock, customer experience, employees, branches etc. A growing business develops a unique brand to differentiate it from the competition and never stops talking about itself and its products. All leading brands in the world have never stopped advertizing their products even when nearly everyone knows about them. Utilize every opportunity to talk about your business. It is also one in which expenses are kept within the accepted levels. Every expense must be made with the intention of generating more money for the enterprise.

A growing business can be compared to a parent raising a second child. Because of the challenges faced raising the first child, the parent gains experience and knows what to do and what to avoid in raising the second. It becomes second nature to such a parent because nothing seems new anymore. Anyone running a business therefore must learn lessons from their initial failures and mistakes to support its growth.

     SMALL BUSINESS IS BIG BUSINESS

Children never give up on anything that appeals to them however much you discourage them. This perfectionist mentality of kids is what hastens their mental as well as physical growth. Business people ought to seek ways of doing more everyday than the previous day. The more one does, the more chances are created to generate more money. We grow daily and so should what we do.

Growing up means graduating from being on the receiving end of all that is good to the giving end. A growing business ought to afford looking after its employees and stakeholders better.

A growing business continues setting and meeting higher targets than before. It can be seen from the increased number of employees hired to take care of the increased customers. Growth is shown by increasing sales volumes and wider coverage. A business grows when it is able to deliver services to more areas through different channels.

A growing business learns from its past mistakes, rectifies them and continuously innovates to keep its customers satisfied. It studies its competitors and strives to outcompete them by offering unique but also better services.

A growing business builds its unique brand and consistently rebrands to keep its visibility in the market. It keeps its brand attractive to the customers and aptly responds to customers' feedback. It creates and sustains the "feel good factor" that customers attach to how they are served.

IS INCREASE IN SALES SYNONYMOUS WITH INCREASED PROFITABILITY?

Maximize profits by minimizing costs of operations.

Many people are on top of the moon when they make so much in sales and you cannot blame them. They have generated a lot more money than they did previously. On closer scrutiny, however, they spend more to generate those sales. Let us put this into perspective by analyzing, for instance, what farmers go through. Most of these are very good at calculating how much their harvests are worth but ask them about what it cost them to produce and very few can authoritatively respond.

Profitability is a result of productivity. If you desire to increase your business profitability, you put more focus on the productivity of your workforce and the efficiency of your work processes. Your workforce must do more work effectively and efficiently. Hiring two employees to serve customers that could be served by a single employee is not being productive. The salary you will pay them will be more than the sales they generate.

Set sales targets for all your team members and facilitate them to perform. Every employee must be a sales agent for the enterprise with which they work. It is the duty of every team member to draw customers to their workplace and products offered. We are the representatives of the companies/enterprises we work with and must therefore deliberately help in raising sales.

Regularly evaluate the cost of customer acquisition. Spending a lot of time and money to attract a customer to buy from you does not make economic sense. Develop a budget to do advertizing that is within your means. Know which clientele to target and devise appropriate means of reaching out to them.

Minimizing the cost of operations is the easiest way of ensuring profitability. Being able to allocate adequate work for every employee increases their productivity. Never keep your employees idle or less occupied. Time wasted is a cost of operation because you end up paying for idle time. Also avoid unnecessary transport costs that arise from poor planning. Purchasing stock in bits is very expensive in the long run. You make more money and profits whenever you purchase in bulk. Identify your fast moving products and always ensure your customers do not miss them when they come in.

HOW DOES SMALL BUSINESS BECOME BIG?

Small is the starting point. Define your path into the future

Anything that starts small must end up big. That is the natural way God designed all creations that are living. There might be slow growth but ultimately every creation ought to reach maturity. Only those creations not well taken care of will become stunted.

A small business grows big depending on the deliberate decisions of its management. The management of this business must be conversant with the business vision, mission and objectives for its existence. These three must be geared towards growing the business from where it is to where it is projected to be in the future. If you want to be recognized as a five star hotel, your mission must be to become just that and you will design objectives tailored in that line. Every objective you achieve drives you closer to your overall goal. If you want your presence felt in more than one city, you will deliberately work towards ensuring this happens. If your overall goal is to acquire or operate in bigger premises, find out what ought to be done and do it without fail

.

The management of the business must set short, medium and long term goals for their business to guide its growth. There must be a "roadmap" to show all stakeholders where the final destination is. Everyone must be able to clearly see where the goal posts are if they are to score for their team.

Playing without goal posts loses meaning and can only be for carrying out exercises but not preparing for a competitive game.

Responsibilities of each and every stakeholder must be made clear to every team member to understand and implement. It must be emphasized that each one's goals ought to fit within the overall goal of the enterprise. Whatever is done must be aimed at achieving the overall goal.

When hiring, the right people must be selected for the right positions and facilitated for the enterprise to grow. When you have recruited, it is important that you orient the new team members. This helps to guide their stay and performance at the workplace. Do not rely on an employee's former experience elsewhere. Every enterprise determines how it should be managed through setting up tailor made policies, processes and procedures. It is within your interest to introduce the new staff to how you want work done.

Be known for offering unique services at appropriate prices. Be helpful to customers who come to you and assist those who find it hard to make choices. Everyone who comes to your place of work is either a customer or potential customer. Even when they lack adequate money to purchase from you, treat them well so that when they get the money, you will be their automatic choice. Let all your customers get a customer experience only unique to you and they will be hooked to you for life. Go an extra mile to make them feel appreciated for choosing to bring their money to you instead of taking it elsewhere.

Use every opportunity to interest more people to your business. There is a variety of ways to advertise business these days.

You can choose to go digital, or use short messages (sms), WhatsApp, phone calls, classified adverts in newspapers, flyers, business cards, brochures, tradeshows/expos etc

Do small things in a great way before dreaming of doing the big great things. Do not fret about the small numbers of customers at the beginning. Do the best you can for them and exceed their expectations. These will be your first points of reference about your superb services. They will return for more services and lure others towards your business. Never take any customers you get for granted. They trust you with their money, do not abuse their trust. The way you handle them will determine the pace of your own business growth or collapse. They will direct more people to you or away from you. Ensure that any and all customers coming to you for services feel appreciated and they will refer more people to your business.

When you learn to handle small numbers of customers satisfactorily, you will find it easy to ably handle bigger numbers as you grow.

Do not ignore television and radio advertizing if your target clientele accesses them. Decide how much money your business can afford to channel into this campaign without affecting your cash flows negatively. Compare the number of customers this brings into your business to those brought by other channels of advertizing. Stick to it for as long as it generates more volumes of sales.

Do not forget to request satisfied customers to refer others to you. Always find a way of rewarding loyal customers and those who go out of their way to refer others to you and your business. Network marketing businesses beat us hands down when it comes to attracting new customers to our businesses. Let us learn from them so that we can promote our businesses better. Your services should make customers feel obliged to refer others to you.Business is about the number of customers that hand over their money to you for the services you offer. Focus on building those numbers.

HOW DO BIG BUSINESSES STAY BIG?

A dynamic world needs dynamic citizens. Staying at the top requires more than reaching the top.

Big is a perception issue and is relative depending on who is defining it. What is big to you might actually be small to someone with thicker lenses than yours. And at times, what you consider small is a dream come true for some individuals that have seen themselves progress from pathetic situations to that particular stage. A business can be as big as the stakeholders continue to push for its improvement. Becoming big in business should never be your ultimate goal. Your ultimate goal must be; to become and stay big. Set ambitious but realistic goals in your business but never give in to the temptation to make up the numbers. Short cuts are costly and must be avoided at all costs.

They maintain the blue print that made it possible to become that big. Rather than ignore what worked then, they make improvements on what used to be done during the growing process.

Incorporate new innovations into your operations and update your policies, processes and procedures to align them to what is currently the new normal.

They strengthen their systems to support the weight of their business. A bigger business faces more challenges as it strives to serve more customers.
The more customers interface with your business, the more issues they get to raise. Always have it at the back of your mind that "A rough sea makes a good sailor".

They listen to customer complaints and work towards getting appropriate remedies. A customer is why you open up for business daily. Without them, we are simply wasting time and money in any business we start. How long would you last in your business if no customer used your services or bought your products?

They invest considerable amounts of money and time in research and development of new products. Peoples' interests and preferences change as fast as they get something better than what is available. Bring what is currently trending closer to them and they will support your business.

They never forget to let people know what they do at any given opportunity. It is quite surprising but we receive new customers daily. These never knew we existed or have been getting their services elsewhere. Never assume that everyone knows the reason for your existence as a company. The best brands in the world continue marketing their products even when their sales are quite phenomenal. You must promote and market your business regularly.

They make deliberate moves into new markets and build more strategic partnerships as they do so. They consistently search for virgin markets where competition is not intense. They identify gaps in the markets and provide solutions immediately.

Big businesses lobby for policies that stimulate their businesses. They know that any policies that negatively increase their cost of operation affect their business growth. They will relentlessly pursue the policy makers; engage them in negotiations to ensure that final policies result in more production and productivity.

Point(s) for action

 SMALL BUSINESS IS BIG BUSINESS

Chapter Three
BUSINESS CHALLENGES

HOW DOES BIG BUSINESS RETURN TO SMALL/NIL?

Failing to plan ahead is planning to fail.

The media is sustained by stories. The media tells more of the successful business stories because they bring in the sales. I guess it is because we like reading and hearing about success stories. Failures scare us to the marrow and very few want to even think about possible failure of their own businesses. Most businesses that have collapsed or shrank in size failed to read and respond to the indicative signs in time. Once the laid down policies, processes and procedures are ignored, any business owner must prepare for the downfall of such a business.

Ever wondered why businesses collapse?

An accumulation of business mistakes result in unsustainable losses. Internal leakages must be sorted out immediately they are known to keep the business healthy and able to expand. Business records should accurately show the financial health of the business. These records must always be compared with tangible assets. Records that are never crosschecked against what is actually available are misleading especially if someone decided to concoct them for his/her own interests.

It should be noted that a business does not collapse suddenly. There are always telling signs of a sinking business. Are you finding a difficulty in restocking even after selling off most commodities? Have you given out too many commodities on credit to your customers? Do you have too many bad debts? Are you writing them off or do you have a well laid out plan to enforce repayment? Are you having many of your items expiring before you sell them? Are you having difficulties in paying your bills? Is your inventory reducing but you cannot see where the money from sales is?

Situations such as these are glaring signs that something is going wrong and the sooner they are sorted out, the better. The factors that cause the collapse of a small business are similar to the ones that cause the collapse of a big one.
If your management skills are wanting, it is a matter of "when" rather than "if" your business will collapse.

Sort out whatever problems exist in your business before they become uncontrollable because when they do, the only way your business will go is down.

When the customer shifts allegiance from you, be very worried. Customers will support you for as long as you provide what they need in a way they feel appreciated. Feedback from customers about your services should never be taken for granted. Coming to support your business when they know they will be disappointed by the service is stressing. When you ignore their suggestion about improved service, they simply move on to more responsive service providers. Interact with your customers as much as possible to find out whether they are satisfied by services being offered by the employees because at times they might not come directly to you but keep complaining to the same staff.

You must also keep abreast with what is trending and avail it for your customers. When you fail to adapt to customers' tastes and preferences, the stock will remain in your shelves. Invest time and money to research about your business to know of the changing trends. Pay a visit to your competitors or send trusted individuals to find out what they are doing right.

Do not use or market technologies/products that are no longer widely used. What worked then might not necessarily work as well now.

Why do borrowers lose their property and other securities to banks, financial institutions and money lenders?

Rarely do we spend a day without news on properties up for sale by financial institutions because their clients failed to repay due debts. Banks, on several occasions, blame borrowers for not reading and understanding the terms and conditions under which they acquire loans. They claim borrowers are more interested in getting the money and simply ask to be shown where to sign.

People have a self-conviction and genuine belief that they will easily repay borrowed money. As a result, very few factor in the probability that circumstances might change along the way. When you do not clearly understand how the terms under which you are borrowing will affect your business and your ability to repay with ease, you are courting trouble.

Most borrowers have underestimated the weight of loans on their businesses and overrated their ability to repay loans. Most factors are not held constant in business and several occurrences beyond your control can change the dynamics at any one time.

Banks are mandated to make profit like any other business. That is why they persuade you to take up the loans with "relatively low" interest rates.

     SMALL BUSINESS IS BIG BUSINESS

They prefer that customers borrow at interest rates that are floating and peg the interest rates to the principal amount borrowed. Since interest rates increase more times than they reduce, it is in the best interests of the borrower to negotiate for repayment at a fixed interest rate.

Please always negotiate for the interest payment to be pegged to the reducing balance rather than the principal amount.

Some borrowers concoct figures about sales, profits, expenses and projected growth so that bankers are convinced to give them the required money. If you borrow money on the premise of concocted figures, you surely are heading for trouble. Other borrowers divert the money into projects for which they did not borrow the money. Although some have survived this mistake and gone ahead to repay their loans, most people who divert the money to other uses end up failing to repay.

Some lenders have cartels that are always hovering around and eager to grab property at the first instance of failure to repay. Because these properties are often sold at less than the market rate, organized groups are in the know and always ready to pay for them immediately.

Stories are rife of lenders who have become filthy rich because of ensuring that borrowers do not pay on scheduled time so that they grab properties. Allegations are made of lenders who switch off phones and make themselves unavailable so that borrowers fault on payments. They reappear long after the due date to grab properties.

It is in your best interest as a borrower to ensure that various repayment options and modes are agreed upon with the lender so that you are not caught unawares by the crafty type of lenders.

Loans are good to facilitate growth. Several people have used loans to expand their businesses faster than they could have done without them. They continue to use borrowed money in their businesses without any trouble. A good look at them will tell you that they follow business principles to the dot and they have ensured that their interests are well taken care of. It is not a must that somebody else will take care of your interests, so go on and take care of your interests in whatever you do.

Negotiate for an option to repay more money per instalment than agreed if you get the funds. This reduces your indebtedness faster in case you access some extra money along the way.

A business is small if the effort put in making it productive is very minimal. Most business people are still engaging in artisanal practices where feeding the immediate family is the main focus. Such people believe that as long as the business caters for family needs, there is no need to stress over gaining more customers and creating more work for oneself. They set themselves soft targets they can easily hit rather than having to continuously stress over finding ways of moving faster and higher in their line of work. This is the reason why you will find a tailor in a similar place you used to see him while still a child.

   SMALL BUSINESS IS BIG BUSINESS

Several people have been in the same place doing the same things over and over again without expanding. They are literally in their own comfort zones. They have arrived and are not interested in moving any farther. Does it not surprise you that some adults are still taken care of by their parents even after educating them?

When will they ever realize their potential without diving into the working minefield? If parents do not encourage them to find or start their own work, these adults might stay dependent for as long as the parents allow them to.

Some people fear that expanding their businesses will attract the "wrath" of tax bodies. Most tax bodies lay the greatest emphasis on formal and relatively large businesses. These are easier to follow up and the cost of collecting taxes from them is minimal compared to the very many informal yet operational businesses. Such people prefer to keep getting their "smaller monies" alone rather than sharing "bigger monies" with the tax bodies.

Most of these informal businesses have lost out on big business because they lack the required documentations to enable them deal with established businesses. They are run at the whim of the proprietor which makes them risky to deal with. Any serious business person will ask themselves what would happen if, by ill luck, the proprietor was incapacitated or even died. They are what we could term as "I'm the business and the business is me".

They are more like an unprotected boda boda rider on his motor bike. He is the body of the motorbike and any accident affects him directly and at most times irreversibly. Its sustainability depends upon the continued good health of the rider.

How do you define your business? Are you proud of it or would you rather no one finds you there?

When someone tells me, I own a "ka small" business, it tells me straight away that they lack passion for it and are just doing it probably to generate some extra money which most cannot even quantify. The way you perceive your business determines how much time and resources you are willing to invest in improving its performance. A business will be as small as you take it to be. If you do not treat your business seriously, it will never be a real business.

Do you ever wonder why many ladies with "small businesses" that men do not want to be seen doing are able to look after their families and even take their children to school? Business should never be a hobby but a money generating venture.

These ladies have realized that this is what they can manage and they put every possible effort into making sure that they grow the business over time. They will re-invest the little profits they get into the business, avoid expensive lifestyles, seek help when stuck, pamper their customers, grow and maintain their customer base and will do all it takes to ensure they sell.

     SMALL BUSINESS IS BIG BUSINESS

Ladies are by far better at managing money more responsibly than men because of the many family responsibilities bestowed upon them by God which require them to innovatively work with whatever budget is available. Women tend to worker smarter than men.

WHY DO SMALL BUSINESSES STAY SMALL?

Stagnation is a result of laziness. You are not meant to stay where you are.

It is strange that some business people are more comfortable remaining small than growing into a force to reckon with. They are so used to doing everything on their own terms that expansion presents them with challenges of managing a bigger workforce. They have challenges trusting anyone else but themselves. To them, "it is too much work". Although this is prevalent in most sole proprietorships, the corporate or employed class is guilty of the same behaviour. When they make some substantial amount of money, they invest in businesses to increase their financial security. The mistake most of them make is to spread their money in several small investments. They will buy cows here, buy goats there and some land on which to rear the animals and establish a plantation. This behaviour is akin to how our forefathers managed their enterprises. Their main focus was to own a little bit of several assets or focusing much attention on one enterprise and doing the bare minimum in others. They never believed in putting all eggs in one basket.

The corporate and working classes sometimes dread growth of their side businesses because such growth would necessitate increased supervision. This increased supervision would require them to resign from their full time employment to enable them create more time and mobilize other resources for their own businesses.

However the thought of having to do without the monthly pay check freaks them out. It is here that the difference is made. As the strong take the risks, the weak and faint hearted choose to stay in their comfort zones.

A business is small if the effort put in making it productive is very minimal. Most business people are still engaging in artisanal practices where feeding the immediate family is the main focus. Such people believe that as long as the business caters for family needs, there is no need to stress over gaining more customers and creating more work for oneself. They set themselves soft targets they can easily hit rather than having to continuously stress over finding ways of moving faster and higher in their line of work. This is the reason why you will find a tailor in a similar place you used to see him while still a child. Several people have been in the same place doing the same things over and over again without expanding. They are literally in their own comfort zones. They have arrived and are not interested in moving any farther. Does it not surprise you that some adults are still taken care of by their parents even after educating them? When will they ever realize their potential without diving into the working minefield? If parents do not encourage them to find or start their own work, these adults might stay dependent for as long as the parents allow them to.

Some people fear that expanding their businesses will attract the "wrath" of tax bodies. Most tax bodies lay the greatest emphasis on formal and relatively large businesses. These are easier to follow up and the cost of collecting taxes from them is minimal compared to the very many informal yet operational businesses.

Such people prefer to keep getting their "smaller monies" alone rather than sharing "bigger monies" with the tax bodies.

Most of these informal businesses have lost out on big business because they lack the required documentations to enable them deal with established businesses.

They are run at the whim of the proprietor which makes them risky to deal with. Any serious business person will ask themselves what would happen if, by ill luck, the proprietor was incapacitated or even died. They are what we could term as "I'm the business and the business is me". They are more like an unprotected boda boda rider on his motor bike. He is the body of the motorbike and any accident affects him directly and at most times irreversibly. Its sustainability depends upon the continued good health of the rider.

How do you define your business? Are you proud of it or would you rather no one finds you there?

When someone tells me, I own a "ka small" business, it tells me straight away that they lack passion for it and are just doing it probably to generate some extra money which most cannot even quantify. The way you perceive your business determines how much time and resources you are willing to invest in improving its performance. A business will be as small as you take it to be. If you do not treat your business seriously, it will never be a real business.

     SMALL BUSINESS IS BIG BUSINESS

Do you ever wonder why many ladies with "small businesses" that men do not want to be seen doing are able to look after their families and even take their children to school? Business should never be a hobby but a money generating venture.

These ladies have realized that this is what they can manage and they put every possible effort into making sure that they grow the business over time.

They will re-invest the little profits they get into the business, avoid expensive lifestyles, seek help when stuck, pamper their customers, grow and maintain their customer base and will do all it takes to ensure they sell.

Ladies are by far better at managing money more responsibly than men because of the many family responsibilities bestowed upon them by God which require them to innovatively work with whatever budget is available. Women tend to worker smarter than men.

When you start up something, put all your heart into it and look out for better ways of doing it on a daily basis, have a plan for making it bigger and more profitable. The passion you exhibit for your business is a magnet for customers because they can see the love you have and feel for your business. It, therefore, becomes impossible for anyone to do anything that messes up the love of their life. Where your treasure is, your heart will be.

Never handle your business as a small enterprise. We have heard, not once, that a journey of a thousand miles begins with the first step. Always have a bigger vision of your present business and set yourself bigger targets to work towards. Start small, dream big, as Warren Buffet puts it in his Essays to Berkshire shareholders. Something is small only when you have anything bigger to show. Wake up every day with a passion of making your business bigger and better than it currently is.

When you start up something, put all your heart into it and look out for better ways of doing it on a daily basis, have a plan for making it bigger and more profitable. The passion you exhibit for your business is a magnet for customers because they can see the love you have and feel for your business. It, therefore, becomes impossible for anyone to do anything that messes up the love of their life. Where your treasure is, your heart will be.

Never handle your business as a small enterprise. We have heard, not once, that a journey of a thousand miles begins with the first step. Always have a bigger vision of your present business and set yourself bigger targets to work towards. Start small, dream big, as Warren Buffet puts it in his Essays to Berkshire shareholders. Something is small only when you have anything bigger to show. Wake up every day with a passion of making your business bigger and better than it currently is.

Do you notice how many developments are going on around you?

There is a Rip Van Winkle character in each of us that must always be fought. This is a character who gets surprised about how much the world changed over a period of time.

Do not let things happen around you without your knowledge. Everything that happens affects us in one way or another. Knowing what is happening enables you to prepare yourself for any eventuality. Ignorance is the biggest impediment to self-development.

Having interest in what is going on opens your mind to different opportunities. Utilizing those opportunities is one of the reasons why some people advance in life while those without that alert mind stay where they are. Everything that happens provides you with opportunities if only you take a good look at it. The first to notice and utilize these opportunities will always gain the greatest benefits. Luck is when opportunity meets preparedness.

Expansion brings its own challenges. No wonder some people prefer to stay "small". It is easier to manage a "small" enterprise without a lot of strain. The challenges surface when expansion starts and different dynamics come into play. Although the principles of management are the same, the intensity of their application and attention to detail becomes the make or break point for either the success or downfall of "big" companies.

Like it was before, so it is today. Customer is king in your business. They bring in the money. Inadequacies, errors, system failures and the lacklustre responses to customer complaints result in a build-up of resentment towards the "big" company services unless deliberate efforts are put in place to rectify them in haste. The skill set that manages small businesses has to be retooled and sharpened more because the challenges that emanate from expansion are immense.

Before expansion, it is vital that plans are designed and put in place to adapt to the expected changes. Because an expanding business is in upward movement, the systems and skill set of employees have to continuously be renewed to keep up with the pace of growth.

The increased number of clients results in a corresponding increase in incidences of customer complaints. If your public relations and research and development departments do not up their game, you are on a sure way downhill and in free fall.

When people get tired of complaining without receiving reassurances of improved services and enjoying these promised improved services, they start voluntarily disentangling themselves from your operations. Always remember that a complaining customer gives you the best opportunity to improve your services by pointing out your inadequacies. Woe unto you if a more credible alternative comes into play.

DO YOU KNOW BUSINESS IS A TWO-WAY TRAFFIC JOURNEY?

Your actions and/or inactions determine which way you and your business will go

Just as some small businesses grow into big businesses, the reverse is true. It is important to realize that businesses grow but others do collapse as well. When you go into business with success as your only expectation, reality will hit you hard. It can never be a one way trip to success. Along the way, a number of challenges will shake you (sometimes to the core of your belief system). Just as you start feeling comfortable in your business, you will be shocked by the collapse of a previously reputable firm. Try as they may, the explanations given never make much sense to the lay people.

The lay person sees a big enterprise and imagines that it can never collapse because at face value, everything is going on very well. There is quite alot that goes on behind the scenes to push these businesses to where they are and to keep them there. When those previously followed practices start to be ignored, instead of the profits that used to be generated, losses become the order of the day. Insiders who will be privy to the state of affairs will do their best to keep this information confidential .It is kept confidential in a bid to find a sustainable way of overcoming them. When you see a once reputable business collapsing, know that every effort to redeem the situation was tried but in vain.

There is a captivating television series titled Shark Tank about entrepreneurs pitching for capital investment to venture capitalists in exchange for shares in their businesses. All entrepreneurs have enchanting stories until they start asking them about their sales, operations practices and the value they attach to their businesses.

Only passionate and confident entrepreneurs are clear about their business details. In fact, there is more capital available than good reliable business ideas on earth. It is clear that no investor wants to be associated with businesses with very low or no sales, high operation and production costs. If your sales are not increasing, it is time you went back to the drawing board, looked at the strategy being used (if any) and see how to improve it.

At the end of the day, a business is as good as the sales and profits it is making. Although business is a two-way journey, we should be known more for business growth than business collapse.

Jumping from one business to another is a sign of lack of focus and failure on your part. Business requires time and sustained effort to grow it. Give any business you decide to do ample time and effort. After you succeed at one, you can move on to diversify into new businesses.

Chapter Four

SUPPORTING BUSINESS GROWTH

WHO ARE YOU?

Clearly define who you are and it becomes very easy to pin point you to your desired destination.

How definite is/are your goal(s)?

Saying, I want to be rich in five years is as ambiguous as saying I want to pass my exams. Ambiguous because it does not define what is rich to you or what level of passing you are looking at.

I shall get distinctions in all my course units/subjects or I will have ten million shillings on my account by the end of two years are more definite statements. It is easier to measure the outcome and know whether you have hit the target or not in these objectives unlike the first two which are general in nature. Make sure the targets you set for yourself, staff, children or anyone you relate with have definite numbers and a time frame.

Just imagine if you decided you wanted to go to any place today without anything to do there in particular. You would be able to reach there at any time of your choosing which could make you a bit lazy. If however, you decided you wanted to be there by 8:00 a.m. for a particular activity/appointment, you would be driven to wake up earlier so that you do not miss the activity/appointment.

Always set yourself goals that are specific, measurable, achievable, realistic and time bound (S.M.A.R.T).Avoid general statements that cannot easily be measured if you want to see your desired results realized. When you hit one target, this enables you to focus on hitting or setting another. Always work with the target in your mind.

How competent are you in whatever you do?

There is nothing as captivating as an entrepreneur or business person who knows their trade in and out. They can confidently tell you where they have been, where they are and where they are going. The extent of your knowledge and competence determines which projects or which work you will be hired to do. That is why when you need treatment, you will look for the best doctor there is or that you can afford.

Use the opportunity you get at work to build a wealth of successfully completed projects that you can always refer to in your future dealings.

When asked what projects you have done and completed successfully, you will be able to pin point them with certainty. Do you have any respectable person that can corroborate your claims? Use your time at work to build your capacity and prepare yourself for future engagements. It should never be an issue of just appearing at or being around your workplace waiting for a pay check.

When do you start to matter in society?

Do you realize that people believe in those who matter to them?
People believe in us when our behaviour is considered humane, when we are experienced and competent in what we do or when we impact people's lives positively through what we do. There is need to make or do something, master it and you will then start to matter.

Very many people do similar things but those that matter to anyone are the ones that have mastered their act.

Put all your efforts into mastering what you do and take control of your behaviour towards others. Should there be any obstacles along the way as is the case always, be quick to improvise, adapt and you will certainly overcome. Decide to be a person that matters in all your circles by doing and being the best you can.

Do you as a brand matter to the circles you belong to? Are you contributing towards improving its quality and productivity? If your answer is not yet or not as much, then let your presence be felt because it should matter. Mediocrity is stressful to those around and should be avoided at all costs. No one enjoys interacting with someone who needs pushing around to do anything. We are drawn to people who are quick to see and do what needs to be done whenever they are around us.

Have an initiative to positively change your surroundings, your work and productivity at work and home. Be the best you can be at what you decide to do and you will always stand out from the crowd. More opportunities are given to those who perform exceedingly well beyond what is expected of them. Even when you know what your responsibilities are, there are more rewards to those that do more than they were hired to do.

     SMALL BUSINESS IS BIG BUSINESS

Do you believe in yourself?

How much do you believe in yourself in terms of percentage? It is easier to believe in others than yourself. Let us consider the following scenarios:

There are many motor accidents on the road but this never stops our daily movements. We all fear death but go to sleep every night yet being asleep is no different from being dead. You do not know what is happening in your surroundings while asleep. Very many ladies die while giving birth but many more get pregnant daily. So many people are mistreated on jobs abroad yet many more struggle to go there even illegally.

Do you ever ask yourself what drives the above actions?

Faith that everything will turn out well for us motivates us. Most of us believe that each one of us is blessed and was created to be successful. The problem is that we have very low opinions of our abilities to do anything worthwhile without the supervision of someone else. Those who believe in themselves know that their actions will result in a positive change for very many people apart from themselves. They are not easily scared by circumstances.

Have you noticed that when you smile or wave at someone, they easily reciprocate the same? You have to believe in yourself so much that everyone is attracted into believing in you. If you need to raise your belief, do all it takes to be good at what you do to the extent that you can comfortably discuss issues in your line of work without a necessity to rely on notes always.

HOW DO PEOPLE FEATURE IN THE BUSINESS?

Take good care of people in your business and they will nurture it forever.

There will always be people on the selling and buying sides of any business. All these people on either side of the divide are very vital in the state of any business. These people are the only reason why businesses exist or collapse. These people can be categorized as business owners, customers, potential customers, employees, suppliers, competitors, regulators, financiers, policy makers, etc. Each of these categories has interests in your business and you must understand and take good care of them should you want to remain in business. Because we cannot do business on our own, it becomes vital that our people relationship and management skills are constantly upgraded to satisfy the others' interests. Take good care of people you interact with in your business and they will support your business continuously.

Business problems emanate from failure by their owners to satisfactorily meet stakeholders' needs. As a business owner, take as much time as you can to find out the needs of all stakeholders in your business. Make it your prime job to ensure that as you move towards your goal, stakeholders are happy with your journey. Disgruntled stakeholders will work tirelessly to pull or even push you down. Any business that is people centred will thrive for generations because people support those who support them. We open up our businesses or offices to interact with people as they buy our products or pay for our services.

    SMALL BUSINESS IS BIG BUSINESS

Owners require dividends from the business and business growth; customers/potential customers require affordable quality products and good customer service; employees require adequate salaries, facilitation to do work, chances to advance their careers and good working conditions; suppliers need trustworthy partners; competitors pray for a limping/ struggling business rival; regulators want you to operate legally; financiers want you to be at par with your personal and business finances; policy makers want you to do well so that you pay more taxes and provide more employment opportunities for the unemployed. It is evident that all these players mentioned and many more unmentioned ones have interests in your business. For it to grow, their interests must always be put into consideration.

The more people you interact with in your business, the better chances of growing faster. It is incumbent upon you to ensure that whoever you interact with gets a special good feeling. That special feeling keeps people coming back for your services.

Our interactions should be aimed at building long lasting relationships. It is through good relationships that businesses generate more sales. People deal with those they know more easily than those they do not. All business people have been helped along the way to strive in business. These people have recommended, defended and connected others to businesses of their friends and acquaintances.

Business people who strive to build working relationships with people in strategic positions seldom face insurmountable challenges.

For every challenge they face, they will have someone to help them overcome it. Because their networks are spread wide, sorting out any issue that arises becomes quite easy and less expensive.

As you attract more people into your business lives, you must be cognizant of the fact that not everyone comes with goodwill. Systems ought to be put in place to keep in check any saboteurs who may infiltrate your circles.

WHY SHOULD EVERYONE OWN A BUSINESS?

Everyone who owns a business understands why their maximum input in any work is demanded.

When will you start minding your own business?

As you work for others, remember that they did not put up the business to make you rich but rather to enrich themselves. Because of this, they will spend as little as possible to keep you on the job while you make more money for them.

Whereas the employers' intention is to ensure you make more money for them, your target as you work there should be to use whatever salary or wages you receive from your employer to start and grow your own business. As you work for others, take keen interest in how they handle employees, customers and colleagues. How do they plan execution of work and how do they build teams that execute any available work? If you are observant and interested in learning, you will learn.

All the above are lessons that will help you as you start up your business. They become more important when you do not have enough time to attend to the daily operations of your business yet you must rely on people working for you. While you keep complaining of little pay at your work place, some of your colleagues have made use of that little pay to generate more money through starting up their personal businesses. Quit giving excuses for your failure to do something worthwhile with your pay and instead find out how your colleagues manage to do it with similar pay.

Will you survive the current downsizing, mergers and closures of businesses?

Most of the people with whom we interact work for others as employees because they fear to venture into business of their own. They prefer to train from other people's businesses as they prepare to start theirs. It should be noted that business owners will always be better off than those they employ. However much you complain for increments, they will never come unless the business owner sees more benefits out of you.

If you are lucky to get employment, use your time there to learn as much as possible. What you learn at work is what comes in handy when you decide to start and run a business of your own. Build your own network to continuously relate with as you perform your duties. These people easily recognize you when you go seeking their help in your own business.

Even as you work, never be comfortable till you develop an exit strategy. There are a number of circumstances under which a job can be lost. Whatever happens, ensure you have a fall back position to absorb the shock of losing your precious job. There are no sentiments/emotions in the hiring and firing processes. Somebody is tasked to do that task and will be required to do it as and when necessary.

A lot is happening in the world of business that we must be alert to how it might affect us. Downsizing, mergers and closures point to one glaring truth: loss of jobs. The economic trend is such that many enterprises are out to reduce their costs of operations while increasing their profitability.

In reducing the cost of operations, workers unfortunately get to be affected first. Automation of systems, combining of closely related positions and doing away with locations, positions and persons that bring less or no value to the enterprise become the main focus of management in a bid to re-engineer targeted profitability. Survival of any employee depends on the added value they bring to the enterprise. The more valuable will be given additional responsibilities whereas those with minimal value will be offloaded. Purpose to position yourself in such a way that whatever change comes on board, you must be in the group to effect the new way of doing things. Do not be negatively affected by the changes but rather be among those to effect the changes.

Doing personal business is very good for anyone out there. The simple reason is that it enables one to understand what goes on in the background before people see the results. You come to appreciate that every small step and person along the chain matters for the desired objective to be achieved.

Never despise or underestimate any person that contributes in any small way towards achieving your set goals. It also teaches us that there are things we cannot do because of our status or simply because we have no idea of how to do them rightly.

You need to realize that employers are more comfortable with responsible employees. These are employees who know that the enterprise's performance is affected by their actions or inaction. They put in extra effort, show high commitment levels, are innovative, patient, are team players ,find out what needs to be done and do it without much pushing and pulling and have a never give up attitude.

WHICH BUSINESS SHOULD I INVEST IN?

People can advise but the ultimate decision is in your hands. The profits and/or losses affect you personally.

There is no clear-cut formula that applies to everyone on how to determine which business to invest in. There are guidelines to help us understand ourselves and what we can do in line with our personalities and interests. Since every business depends on the owner for its performance, their conduct is key in shaping the affairs of running the business.

How does one identify opportunities for business investment?

With the widespread opportunities for making money, most people are still not sure which ones to get involved in. Several sources of investment worth consideration include the following:

Consider the skills you have developed over time and start a business that can rely on these skills to serve people and make money for yourself.

What talents do you have or better still what are your hobbies? A whole lot of opportunities abound in this from personally developing your talent and those of others.

What needs/problems in your community need to be addressed? Every community has an unmet need or faces unique problems. Address these and you have a business to generate money for you.

What resources in your possession are underutilized or redundant? There is nothing that is useless on earth. Find ways of utilizing resources you have access to either to increase their productivity or put them to use.

What qualifications do you possess? How experienced are you in what you currently do? Use these to support a business that requires these two?

In all that you do, what gives you the most satisfaction besides getting paid to do the work? Passion for what one does plays a cardinal role in the success of any business. Determine what you enjoy doing even without payment and lay strategies to make money out of that passion.
Several opportunities and ideas are discussed or promoted in exhibitions, trade shows, print and broadcast media, catalogues and in several social media platforms on a regular basis. It is important that we seek for investment information in several fora to help us make informed decisions.

Never ignore the strength of brainstorming within networks you belong to. A lot of ideas from these networks have been turned into profitable businesses by those keen enough on doing more focused research. The brainstorming provides one with competing opinions and facts about why an opportunity might succeed or not. Research will enable you most times to make your own decision about the said opportunity.

As you ponder on which opportunities to invest in, it is vital for you to know that management of any investment is the number one driver of success or failure of any venture.

You do not need to be a doctor to own a hospital or health facility and neither should one be a teacher to own a school.

What is important is that you know and understand how the system you want to invest in runs. Once this system has been established and the right people hired, you will be able to do any business successfully.

Looking around us, we see investors with a chain of investments for which they lack professional qualification. They have built supporting systems to run these businesses. Build your capacity to manage businesses by interesting yourself into what it takes to run a business successfully. You can never run away from practicing business principles in any venture. Go by them and you are assured of success. Avoid or ignore them and failure will stare you in the face.

Just when people are puzzled about which business to do, others start without even asking anyone for an opinion. Once they believe in an idea, they won't be swayed by anyone's negative opinion. What matters to them is the fact that others are doing a similar business and are not quitting. Business people will always complain about low sales and yet they won't quit.

The most authentic appraisal of your ability to manage a business is that carried out by yourself. Have an honest assessment of your strengths and weaknesses. Build on your strengths and put in place mitigation measures for your weaknesses.

 SMALL BUSINESS IS BIG BUSINESS

All business people have weaknesses but they never allow them to weigh down their full potential. They partner with those strong in areas where they are weak.

Any business will generate adequate money for as long as there are fewer people engaged in it. The more people join the market, the lower the sales and hence profitability. Look at the mobile money market as it currently is. The outlets are becoming as many as the shops in any one area. Every shop with a veranda free of merchandise will sub-let it to a mobile money agent to transact from there. The end result is having so many mobile money agents serving the same number of customers. While the customers are happier because of getting several options, the agents will not easily make enough money to pay their bills.

If you scrutinize their expenses, you realize that most of them are bound to throw in the towel sooner rather than later. Tell me, if you hire the line(s) you are using, pay rent for space, pay rent where you stay, transport and feed yourself and need money to cater for other necessities, how long will you last in an overcrowded business?

A business that is not easy to copy within a short time gives one ample time to make "handsome" profits before others come into play. Identify a need/problem in the community that requires a solution but with few service providers or none. Never enter a saturated market. You will be merely in busyness rather than business. You cannot go wrong with a business that has many customers but fewer competitors. Identify that and you are in big business.

So many options to consider that I cannot easily decide. What do I do?

There are two things that confuse all of us in life and we are yet to agree by consensus. What business should I do? How much money is needed to start? Some of us will know or think they know what they want to do but then the challenge is the zeroing on the amount of money needed to start. Others have accumulated some money but are yet to decide upon what business to engage in. A look at any particular place is evidence of a multitude of businesses one can do if they made a decision to join the race for money generation.

Man was created with an appetite for nearly everything that appeals to the eye and mind. You can sell anything under the sun and customers will come. Some are even eagerly waiting for something from the sun. They like being the first to do or possess anything new.

A number of us get an analysis- paralysis once we are presented with many options. We want everything yet it is practically impossible. You cannot do everything in life because life is about choices. Build your capacity to make the right choices. Any choice is right once you acknowledge your role in making it work. There are several people making it big in all areas we despise or that we fear diving into.

Someone has done it before; you can do it too and do it better. You have money, use it to generate more. You do not have money, do work to accumulate it. Money is an enabler to making life enjoyable. Do not be comfortable without money

As you are thinking of what to do, someone is generating money right at this moment. What you fail to make is made by others ready to take the step. Avoid having idle money around you. Let it work as well. Take that first step, thank me when you do.

Anything that is legal and has demand can be turned into a business. What makes it a business is sustained demand and supply. Once you decide to start something, ensure you prepare yourself for the long haul. Do not do things with short term goals only. You must develop short, medium and long term goals. Achieving short term goals must lead to realization of the overall long term goal.

It is, however, vital to realize that not all innovations are a reaction to demand from the population. Several products on the market have been as a result of a well-orchestrated plan to create demand for them. A product can be introduced into a market and continuously marketed till everyone is enticed into giving it a try. The hype around some products is adequate to convince members of the public that it is worth associating with. As you come up with this product, ensure that it is able to solve a prevailing challenge or eases life for the user.

How should we turn the ideas we have into profitable businesses?

Ideas are useless unless turned into something productive.

We all have several ideas at any particular time but seldom turn them into profitable businesses because of a number of reasons and sometimes excuses. There is no single vehicle that can lead you to developing a profitable and sustainable business. Equal emphasis must be given to a number of factors that can be considered drivers or vehicles used to turn ideas into businesses.

When is the right time and how long should one wait?
An idea whose time has come is easy to turn into a profitable business. A look into several innovations over time shows that each era comes with its own innovations. Studying the trend of business enables us to start businesses that will last. Many innovations have become obsolete as times go by and advanced technology gets used to solve prevailing challenges.

Give your ideas time to grow. What stalls most people from turning their ideas into businesses is a lack of patience necessary in entrepreneurship. As time progresses, our ideas get fine tuned into clearer and workable projects. Do not think of something and just go ahead to invest in it before making sure it is something you are willing to spend the rest of your life doing.

A decision about when to turn any idea into a running business must be made by anyone serious about earning an income from that idea. Develop a timeline for all your intended activities meant to enable you kick start your business. Start developing your idea as soon as it crops up in your mind. Think about a number of options of turning it into a running business.

What skill sets do you have at your disposal?
Whatever we do requires requisite skills to be accomplished. Before deciding about which idea you intend to turn into a business, ensure you are skilled in that area or have skilled labour force to sustain it. Those without requisite skills invest in hiring skilled people to produce the quality acceptable in the market. What you should however ensure is the fact that you must be competent to supervise your workforce. Management is where most businesses go wrong. Build your capacity to manage your investments by taking up appropriate courses specifically designed for people like you. No one will look after your business better than you because it is your life.

You are the vision bearer and therefore must inspire your employees to work hard towards your dream. Management of employees and business demand a different kinds of skills than actual work. Management deals mostly with people skills whereas work skills are mostly technical in nature. How you handle people you work with and for determine the level of success of your business.

What does your market research tell you?
The market will always support anything that solves prevailing problems and/or makes life enjoyable. Any idea must be tested in the market to determine how economically viable it is. Ask a lot of questions from a target group of people to get feedback about your intended innovation. These are the people who will be utilizing this innovation after all and their feedback will help you understand how to present it. The bigger the sample and the wider the area covered the better and more representative your research will be. Find out what your cost of production and operations will be. What are the comparative prices for similar products or close substitutes? Which categories of people buy similar products and why do they prefer them? What is the growing trend in the market? Is the market saturated or is it virgin in terms of what you want to introduce?

How unique is your branding?
This is an activity of giving a particular name and image to goods and services so that people will be attracted to them and want to buy them.

Whatever you do must be easy for people to relate to you. Introduce a unique product in a unique way. There will always be very many products serving a similar purpose in the market but your survival depends on the response of people to your product. If they feel good when using your product or when being served, they are more likely to support you on a sustainable basis. Have the satisfaction of customers at the back of your mind whenever you introduce any product on the market.

People who are hooked onto a brand never buy any other product. They develop brand loyalty because of the derived satisfaction. A careful discernment of products on the market shows us which brands are sought after more than others. Producers of these renowned brands insist on the highest of quality for all products they release onto the market and customers trust them for this attention to detail.

As you introduce any product onto the market, commit yourself to developing and sustaining the highest quality possible for your customers' satisfaction. Make your product known far and wide by using various media to reach your target customers. Let customers come face to face with your products and advertising materials wherever they turn.

Have repeat customers appraise the performance of your products and recommend them to others. People who have utilized products over a long time are more believable than any marketing information producers and/or employees put out.

How much capital do you need?
Capital is the single most challenge every entrepreneur seems to complain about. Some lack adequate capital to scale up their operations to their satisfaction yet many more claim they lack start-up capital.

Unique ideas attract loads of capital compared to the ordinary ones. This must confirm to all of us that capital is available to those who can prove that their ideas are viable and unique. Money attracts more money.

If your idea has a great chance of providing a return on investment, people will be enticed to invest in your idea.

Capital is what enables us to implement our plans. Plans without a backing of funds simply remain on paper. Ensure that whatever plan you come up with has a budget for implementation purposes.

After drawing up a budget for start-up and operational expenses, find ways of mobilizing these funds to enable you turn your plan into a running business. Inadequate capital is as challenging as too much of it at the beginning of the business. When capital is inadequate, the business will be wobbling. Too much capital, on the other hand, keeps our focus away from efficiency. Most people tend to imagine that money can solve every challenge that crops up. Too much capital gives one false comfort that everything worth paying for will be catered for. Owners of most start-ups will even be tempted to reward themselves with hefty salaries at the expense of injecting the money in building the business.

Which virtues should we develop and maintain in business?

Shortcuts in business are not sustainable. Know but also implement best practices in business.Values/virtues imparted into us determine our performance of duties.

People who have cut an edge in business have a tendency of following similar principles. They have been in business for long and realize what keeps or breaks businesses. They have nurtured their strengths and found mitigation measures against their weaknesses.

There are several behaviours or attitudes that most people take for granted yet mean a lot for the survival and sustainability of any venture. An interaction with successful business minds will teach one several lessons about what most of us lack. Whereas most of us complain of lack of capital, you will learn that capital is useless without a number of disciplines. Any amount of capital in the hands of a person who lacks these disciplines soon goes to waste. There are several of them but for this book I have chosen to highlight the following lessons:

What is your vision?

Anyone dreaming of becoming successful must have a clear vision of what future they are working towards. It does not matter how small your business currently is. You will only go as far as you commit yourself. Successful people always have short, medium and long term goals to fulfil. What they do presently is designed to enable them to fulfil their long term goals.

Successful business people go after everything they dream about with a lot of determination. They never allow anything to stand in the way of achieving their set goals. They keep at it till accomplishment. They are fully focused on turning their ideas into reality.

Do you have self belief?

Do you believe in yourself? Everyone will try to tell you why it is not possible and how so and so failed at it. Listening to a wide variety of views concerning your intentions is desirable but what you do about them is up to you.

Successful people have total belief in themselves and what they do. They never allow negativity to cloud their focus. They use criticisms to prepare more and focus on those areas of concern. Criticisms stir them into action to prove naysayers wrong. They will go to the moon and back if necessary to ensure their plans are put into productive action.

They know and understand that they must make the ultimate choice and pay the ultimate price for their dreams. No one else is or will be blamed for any failures in your life. Amidst all challenges and saboteurs, you are totally responsible for keeping the belief in yourself and doing what you believe to be the right thing to do.

How much passion is in you?

We are all individually enthusiastic about something. We spend the bigger part of our lives doing certain things because we are simply attached to them. The happiest of us engages in activities they are passionate about. This passion is a strong love for specific activities.

Passion keeps us pushing against all odds because we feel contented when doing what makes us happy. Choose something you are passionate about and turn it into a money generating activity. Money easily follows the passionate. People easily give you business when they realize how passionate you are about serving them and satisfying their needs.

What are your commitment levels?
Every one of us respects people who are committed to their work. When you decide or agree to do something, focus on it till completion. When someone chooses you, they trust you will offer impeccable services. How committed you are to your work determines the quality of your results. Committed people accomplish tasks in time and do not need constant supervision and checking on. They understand that accomplishing their tasks in time unlocks a lot of potential for others.

Do you know your value?
We exchange money for value. Most of us have been taken advantage of by people supposed to support our growth and development. We have done work for which we were paid peanuts or nothing at all afterwards. While starting out, we rarely know our actual value and are even scared of asking for a fee for offering our services.

Successful people have determined their real value and ensure they are paid for the work they do. They offer voluntary services but at their own discretion. They offer voluntary services or offer services at subsidized charges with an intention of opening up long term working relationships.

Long term working relationships generate more money for those involved for as long as they are handled well. Agree on your price before going out to work. Agree on your working terms and conditions early enough in your interactions with clients.

How do you rate yourself in time management?
Time is something we never seem to have enough of. Whereas we spend a lot of time working, we waste much more in useless activities that never add economic value to our lives. If you are to build a big business, you have to invest a lot of time in activities meant to drive the business forward. Successful people will report to work earlier than the rest and depart later than everyone else. They will even spare additional time for the business when and if necessary.

They use whatever time available optimally. They will openly tell you, they have no time to waste. There is no idle time for them. When their work is done, they take on other tasks and/or search for other opportunities that may generate money for the business.

Can people vouch for your excellence at work?
To get and sustain customers, we must commit to being excellent at whatever we do. People support businesses that satisfy their needs. When you solve peoples' challenges, you become relevant to them. It becomes important that we keep improving the standards of what we do as peoples' tastes and preferences change very often. Building lasting brands requires that whatever we do meets the highest of standards.

We can only compete favourably if our products meet the sector standards. You cannot cut an edge as a big business by doing shoddy work. Soon your time run out and you will be out of business.

Does reliability come naturally to you?

Everyone can produce and/or deliver any product they set eyes on. Most business people start with a lot of verve only to lose momentum along the way. Sustaining production and standards become challenges for most start-ups. All start-ups have challenges of reliability. They get overwhelmed with demand for their products and services. Whereas all start-ups fight hard to gain acceptability in the public, they fall short on reliable supplies.

Anyone dreaming of starting a lasting business must commit to being reliable. Failing to sustainably produce and/or supply required products distorts the market. Nothing hurts business relationships like breaching a long-term supply contract. Build working relationships with people doing a similar business and if possible, agree upon a memorandum of understanding to define how to fulfil bigger contracts that none of you can satisfy alone.

Are you exemplary?

As the vision bearer, all employees and other stakeholders look upon you to drive the venture forward. What you do easily rubs off everyone involved. Telling people to do what you do not do is not effective because they think you are incapable of doing it yourself. Employees are like kids who imitate what parents do. Consistently reporting late to work demotivates your staff who are used to reporting early

. If you want your team to commit to work, you have got to be committed yourself. Teach them the values you want them to uphold while performing their duties. Let them see you working much more than they do.

Do you understand the importance of humility?
Being a boss does not mean you should be bossy. You earn more respect from your team by being humane. Being easily approachable helps you to know everything that goes on and rectify any problem that arises quickly. If possible, spare some time to talk to as many employees as possible and while at it, ask them about their impression of the operations of the enterprise.

Use this feedback to seek clarification from their immediate supervisors with a view of improving the work conditions.

Do not promote fear at the workplace because it is detrimental to the team's productivity. Having employees running around because the boss has arrived is not a good sign. You should earn your staff's respect other than cultivate fear in them. Working out of fear affects their productivity and innovation. They never seem to consider themselves part of the enterprise. They feel threatened and lack job security.

Are you a proponent of teamwork?
Teamwork is the number one driving factor for all results. Businesses that have teamwork invest a lot of time in capacity building. Every team member plays a huge role in contributing to the overall goal of the company. Failure to do one's part fails the entire team.

Productivity can only be sustained through focused teamwork. Any business is as good as the team running it.

Do you hold your employees' hands?
Every business has a unique way of operating. Some employees are hired when they have never worked anywhere else. Others have an experience of working at a different place. It is vital that new employees are taken through an orientation to enable them understand your way of doing things. They perform better when they know how you want your work done. Keep mentoring and coaching them as long as they are with you. It takes time for a person to turn out as perfect as you want them.

How do you rate your financial discipline?
Anyone without financial discipline is bound to encounter numerous problems in the community. They are always at fault with others. Money is the cause of most disagreements at work and between partners. It is vital that one learns to live within one's means by limiting their expenses to only the necessary ones. Not everything out there is for you to spend money on. Separate personal money from business money. Use the money you earn from the business to cater for your personal needs. Let business money cater for business expenses and re-investment.

Ensure that business money caters for budgeted items. Pay for work that is only perfectly completed. Ensure there is value for money always. Maximize sales and minimize costs. This allows the business to have adequate working capital.

Do you support research and development?

Businesses meant to last long invest in continuous research to keep abreast with the changing times. Innovations only come up when you focus on improving what is available or searching for solutions for prevailing challenges. Study the trend within your sector and develop products that add value to peoples' lives.

Do you carry out continuous marketing?

It is only through marketing that most people will know what you do and what you produce. Never rely on word of mouth only. Use every available medium to talk about your products. The farther your message goes, the more demand you create for your products. Searching for markets should be a daily challenge and not a onetime event. Empower all your employees to market on behalf of the business. Make serving more customers in more places a lifetime goal.

What strategic partnerships are you in?

Successful people relate with others who add value to them and their businesses. They develop a working relationship with them. Avoid time wasters in your business and personal life interactions. Strive to understand what determines your business growth and befriend decision makers in the different sectors. If possible, build a personal relationship with them long before you might need their help.

Have you identified forward and backward linkages?
Any business venture you engage in ought to have forward and back linkages. Ensure there is a value chain for your businesses with several operators depending on each other. At what stage of operations do you come in?

Develop a healthy working relationship with everyone involved in the value chain of your business. You need everyone at different stages of your operations.

How do i get necessary capital?

Capital is all around us but is attracted by our preparedness and actions.

Most times when we cannot do something, the first excuse will be about lack of adequate money. Do you ever wonder why even with sufficient money, enterprises still struggle to survive in the dynamic business environment? Most times it is not about the money but management of the different components vital for proper functioning of the business.

How do you perform in your role and how do you help others perform better? How do you develop and maintain good working relationships in your enterprises? How do you mobilize and manage the necessary resources to achieve your objectives? How do you handle the results of your operations? Best management practices are key to the success of any business. Consider money after ensuring that necessary plans for execution are in place. Sometimes it is not all about money but rather how prepared you are to use the resources all around you. Money is one of the vital resources that must be managed well in order to succeed in life.

What have you so far done in pursuit of achieving the targeted outcome? What have you achieved viz a` vis the targeted outcomes?

Chances for funding are higher when you can prove that you have been actively working towards achieving the desired outcome rather than if you want funding to kick start the process.

How much of the total budget will you or your group cover? It is advisable that you mobilize resources of your own to help you kick start the project. It makes more sense if you are willing to invest your own money and time in the project you are seeking funding for.

Of what benefit is your project to the community? Projects with benefits to the community are more likely to be funded than those with personal benefits. What makes you the best person/group to implement this project? What is unique about you or your group that no one else can implement the project the way you intend to?

How reasonable is your budget for the proposed project? Because we shop in the same markets, most of us know the prevailing prices for commodities. Where we do not, finding out is very easy. Exaggeration of prices is an indication of dishonesty. How would you deal with a dishonest person?

Before submitting your proposal requests for funding, you ought to have answers to the questions above and follow proposal guidelines from funding agencies.

What are bankable projects? What determines your ability or inability to get loans from banks? Banks consider several factors before lending money lest they make a loss.

Your honest answers to the following questions will enable you to gauge your chances of accessing funding.

Is your business legal and registered?

Is the security you want to offer legit and more valuable than the money you are requesting for? Does the business have a sound and competent management running it? Does it have proper records of accounts? Does it show a consistent growth in terms of sales and profits? Is your business a start-up or has it been operational for a long period of time?

How do you handle funds received? How do you behave when you receive funds? Do you bank them immediately or do you bank some and spend some at source? How often do you bank and withdraw? How much account balance do you maintain?

What other sources of income do you have? Will you be able to repay the loan in case your project fails or delays to become profitable? Is your business tax compliant? Do you pay all relevant dues in time? Have you clearly spelt out what you want to use the money for, how you will do it and the intended outcome?

     SMALL BUSINESS IS BIG BUSINESS

How reasonable are your budget figures?

Anyone that requires money to kick start any business ought to be trusted in the first place. They should have a proper background of utilizing money availed to them. Any proof of prior misuse repels money. Mobilize your own money before seeking help from any other person. Do not go seeking for funding when you have none of your own. Do not underestimate your ability to generate money of your own. It only requires you to understand that you need money to achieve your targets. It thereafter becomes easier for you to do any activities that bring in money as long as they are legal.

Family, friends and well-wishers are the second sure source of funding for any money generating activity. Most of them will not even require that you pay an interest on borrowed money. They know you quite well and would want you to prosper and help others as well. When you prosper, you help your siblings, the family and most times the extended family benefits as well. If you cannot convince these ones, then you need to check yourself and your idea. Use their feedback to fine tune your idea and seek funding from other sources or think of something else altogether.

Look around your premises for any idle/ redundant or out-of-fashion items that you no longer use frequently. Sell these off to generate money that you so badly need. There is a lot of money locked up in items we no longer use. Ask those you stay with for permission to dispose of such items.

Have you ever thought of being paid upfront before delivery or upon delivery? If you are a trader, find out the prices of items of your interest, take photos of these items and look for buyers. Take these items to customers at a slightly higher price. If you are into contractual works, ensure that you are paid between 50-70% of the contract price before undertaking any work. Design arrangements for instalment payments due to you in such a way that they enable you to carry out your customers' work smoothly.

Talk to suppliers and agree upon terms of payments for items taken on credit. Every seller wants goods out of their premises as soon as possible. Often times, they are willing to sell them out on credit. Develop a healthy relationship with your suppliers so that they can trust you with their products. Pay them on due dates to keep this relationship sustainable.

When you start operations, ensure that you re-invest profits to increase the working capital at hand .Re-invested profits accelerate business growth.

Another financing option is surrendering a stake of ownership to an investor in exchange for a money contribution. The investor gets to own a percentage of your enterprise and you get money to run the business. Some investors will be comfortable with you running the business with less interference from them whereas others demand to have a say in how it is run. Whereas both investors will expect dividends at the end of the year, it is up to you to decide which one adds more value to your business.

Not all financing must be on cash basis. Some commercial banks deal in lease financing. Leasing, instead of purchasing equipment, is a cost-effective way of managing your cash flow more effectively. By leasing, you pay predictable, regular monthly instalments as opposed to a single lump sum. This allows you to fund other areas of the business with less funds available. When you sign a lease, the leaseholder (bank in this case) owns the equipment and avails it to you for use in exchange for the lease payments you make. Visit any commercial banks that provide this service to discuss their terms.

Get rid of money draining behaviours in your life. Why pay exorbitant rent when you can comfortably reside in an affordable smaller yet presentable house? Why buy an expensive vehicle that needs daily maintenance before you are financially secure? Why even buy a vehicle while still renting? Live within your means so that you can save money to channel into investments of your dreams. Alot of money can be mobilized from resetting our priorities. Everything you want is not necessarily what you need to prosper in life. Let your expenses be driven by needs rather than wants. Let us all focus on buying what generates more money for us or what does not drain our earnings endlessly.

Do you have any strategic partnerships?

Nothing succeeds without working in partnership with others. You alone are insufficient.

Because we are in this world as a people, we must work with them in whatever we strive to achieve. Customers, suppliers, competitors, regulators, owners, employees, business partners are some of the vital stakeholders in the businesses we do and we must find a way of working with in pursuit of our goals.

Do you know your most important stakeholders?

We are in the business of looking for money on a daily basis but very few of us are aware of the stakeholders who can make or break our businesses.

All we do is focus on ourselves and make everything about us. We make the primary role of being in business about our own survival forgetting that we are just one part of a complex inter connected system. As we do our businesses, we ought to identify and work with the stakeholders involved. Stakeholders, in simple terms, are those people or entities influenced by our being there or those who influence our continued stay in progressive business. Anyone in business or thinking of joining the business world must take keen interest in a number of stakeholders. I will highlight just six who are the cornerstone of our wellbeing:

1: Business owners

These are people who bear the vision of any business they decide to bankroll. They know where the business must go and mobilize necessary resources to smoothen this journey. They bear the biggest responsibility for the success or failure of this business. They enjoy the biggest percentage of all profits generated. Losses strike them harder than any other stakeholder. Because everything about the business rotates around and about them, anyone working in a business must understand that their continued stay in their positions is hinged on how adequately they address the owners' projections and fears.

2: Customers

These are people who bring money to the business in exchange for the services and goods offered. They literally oil the business engine. They are the life support for our businesses. The customers you serve every passing minute translate into your total earnings.

Every business person's number one job is to attract and retain as many customers as they can handle satisfactorily. Social media has opened up a whole new world of letting people know what services one offers. Simply opening up shop and waiting for customers to come to you is archaic and it, alone, no longer brings the much needed numbers of customers to sustain a business.

Go out to where customers are so that you can add onto the numbers you already have. Provide the services they need and make them feel appreciated for choosing you.

The way you handle them and make them feel is as important, if not more important, as the products and services you present to them.

3: Employees

These are the backbone of any business. They do what you can do and what you cannot do. They are the face of your business because customers interact with them more than they do with business owners. The way they handle customers determines whether they will do business with you or not. Employees know you are the boss so stop rubbing it down their throats whenever you feel like. Stop threatening them with dismissals and pay cuts for wrongs they do while performing duties but rather mentor and coach them to achieve the goals of the business.

Train your employees; give them job descriptions, treat them humanely and pay them a commensurate salary. A motivated workforce is more productive than a disgruntled one. Make them feel that working in that business is the best thing that could ever happen in their lives. Let them feel like they miss something whenever they do not come to work.

4: Bankers

Anyone serious about getting into and staying in business must understand how important bankers are in and for your business. It is imperative that we develop working relationships with banks and bankers. Having business accounts plays a very big role in enabling business people separate business from personal expenses.

     SMALL BUSINESS IS BIG BUSINESS

Big spending entities only deal with businesses that have business accounts. Spending cash is discouraged by most business entities because it becomes harder to track cash flow.

Give your business an identity by opening and maintaining an active business account. Getting notable works requires one to have an active business account. Financiers for any business/project will demand to scrutinize verified bank statements of your business.

The business cash flow and its management tells quite a lot about the health of the business and the competence of those running it. Money should not only be withdrawn from your accounts. Do businesses that enable you to deposit money into your account regularly.

5: Regulators

There is nothing we do under the sun that does not require regulation. If we were left on our own, a lot of unacceptable practices would be carried out. As we do or intend to do business, let us make it a point to interact with the different regulators in our sectors. Let us empower ourselves with knowledge of the requirements of running our businesses and abide by set regulations. Knowing that your business is regulated by a sector authority gives the different stakeholders we deal with confidence about the quality of your products and/or services.

6: Tax Authorities

Countries are largely run on money generated from citizens and non- citizens who pay taxes. Prior to lobbying for loans and grants from abroad, citizens are obliged to pay taxes so that governments have adequate financial muscle to deliver quality services to citizens and non- citizens living in the country.

Seek to understand your tax obligations and contribute to building the nation. Lobby legislators to pass legislations that widen the tax base and reduce the tax burden on the few that pay them. Demand for legislation that promotes fair taxes spread across board rather than targeting the few who do business legally.

Some entities that are capable of offering you life changing business opportunities require tax clearance certificates to prove that you operate legally and fulfil your obligations towards the country in which you operate. Paying taxes is therefore not only good for the country but your business as well.

Chapter Five:
SUCESSION PLANNING

BUT IS BUSINESS NOT RISKY?

Everything in life is risky. Not doing business is risky too. Which risk would you rather live with?

Do you know why people prefer to buy from people they know? It is very vital that we build relationships with several service providers as well as personal relationships with people that work there. I have noticed in several organizations that people who are personally known to employees or their bosses are treated differently from those that are unknown.

I was recently discussing a potential business opportunity with a client who deals in phone power banks and other electronics. I asked why there is a wide disparity in prices for the power banks on the local market. He taught me something new; the capacity of some power banks is lower than what is inscribed on them. As a result, they have products to cater for the various price ranges of their customers.

You will find a 10,000mAh capacity power bank that, on close scrutiny, is actually 4,000mAh being sold on the market. People well known to you will think twice before giving you a product whose quality they are not sure of because they risk losing your trust and relationship. When they are not sure of the product, they are more likely to tell you the truth beforehand.

What is the difference between risk and risky in investments?

When driving or riding on the road, there is always a risk of an accident occurring at any one time. Driving with your hands off the steering wheel is however riskier. Riding like boda bodas on rampage is the riskiest.

A boda boda rider moving with hands and sometimes feet free of the motor bike or even moving on one tyre is something that never ceases to amaze me.

The irresponsibility of these motorists who most times lack protective wear is way too incomprehensible. It is vital to note that the behaviour of motorists on the road increases or decreases the risk of accidents happening.

Whereas mitigation measures can be developed against risks, it becomes difficult to develop these measures for someone who deliberately engages in risky behaviour. Mitigation measures allow you a level of control in minimizing the impact but risky behaviour diminishes this control.

Most people fear investing their money because of the risk of losing it. It is risky to invest in something you have no idea about. We live at the time of the information age where information can easily be found online, in print and broadcast media, the investment environment is no longer as risky. Focus on investments you are passionate about. Having experience in an investment area of your interest reduces your risks. Educate yourself about the investments of your interest by searching for relevant information to enable you make informed decisions.

Talk to more experienced people (than you) in your area of interest. Learn from those who have travelled the journey you are starting. Take lessons from those that have succeeded in this journey and those that have failed along the way. Interest yourself in financial literacy to enable you understand the set of skills and knowledge vital for making informed and effective decisions regarding money matters.

More importantly, investing is a relationship building venture. Make sure you are comfortable with the people involved in the investments you are interested in. You would not want the unnecessary pull and push scenario due to failure to agree on the direction an investment should take. Investing without taking the above points into consideration is as risky as driving a vehicle with your hands off the steering wheel or the boda boda rider who takes his hands and feet off the motor bike while on the road.

Any investment should have mitigation measures to take care of risks along this journey otherwise it is doomed to collapse.

What are you not being told? What is the news behind the headlines? Never take any information at face value. Some people say one thing yet mean quite a different thing. Make sure you understand what you are being told before you do anything. Do not be mechanical in your interpretation. You owe it to yourself to develop your own opinion about anything and everything. I always listen to people to know what their thoughts and beliefs are and relate them to their actions. If your talk and your actions are in contradiction, I will be very cautious in dealing with you.

Very many people employ reverse psychology in their relationships with others. They will do something so that a targeted person reacts in a way they can take advantage of. Some people are so calculative that they plan in advance what actions to bring on when you react in a certain way. Do not go into business with one eye closed. Both eyes should be in agreement.

Watching, "NOW YOU SEE ME", made me realize how cunning people can be. They can mislead you into the opposite direction of where the actual action is taking place when it suits them. They anticipate your actions and divert your attention elsewhere.

Do not be easy to mislead. Always look out for your interests. How does doing something benefit you and does it fit in your general game plan? Better a little caution than a great regret. Mistakes and failures are part of growth.

What makes you think others are not facing similar challenges as you?

Watching our national football team, The Uganda Cranes play against Mali in the African cup of Nations competitions got me thinking of how far we can go to make excuses for anything. You should have heard fans complaining about how the soggy football pitch had hindered The Uganda Cranes from scoring many goals. What they seemed to ignore is the fact that the Mali team were facing similar challenges on the same pitch.

Every situation demands strategies specific to it and the earlier you adopt and adapt these strategies the better the results. Whoever takes advantage of the new situation has more chances of success than one that fails.

People who ferociously criticized The Uganda Cranes for not scoring in the tournament had an answer in Farouk Miya's wonderful goal. The national team continued to represent themselves and the country well against Mali.

Lack of playing time at that level for goal keeper Odongkara resulted in the team conceding a goal. He lacked the sharpness and quick response of Dennis Onyango while in the goal area.

Geoffrey Massa is one hero we have forgotten very fast. Because we were focused on winning the match, very many fans did not want to see him anywhere near the pitch. This is a player that made us proud in the journey for qualification and everyone sang songs of praise for his performance. The lesson we must learn as a people is that history is considered relevant in as much as it supports what is currently happening. Your performance will always be judged in the present and not in the past. Everyone must strive to be better every day because you are as good as your last performance.

As you complain of unusual challenges you must acknowledge that very many others go through the same. It is upon you to devise appropriate means of overcoming the challenges before you. Everyone must focus within themselves to overcome any challenges without excuses because everyone else faces them as well.

As long as you are active, you are bound to make mistakes. Making mistakes is the way we learn of what not to do again. Mistakes are learning experiences which when well utilized can spur more deliberate growth. Our failures and mistakes as well as those of others ought to inspire us to do much better than before. They only become irreversible if we do nothing positive about them. Most of the successful people in life have failed many times but were motivated to do more by the little successes they often attained. Just like it is rare for somebody to return home because of stumbling along the way, business people should never freeze because of failures every now and then.

Do a lot of research about what you do and talk to people more experienced and knowledgeable than you in your line of business. They have walked the journey you are travelling and know quite a lot that could save you a lot of time and money to achieve what you set out to do.

IS ACTIVITY SIMILAR TO PRODUCTIVITY?

Toddlers and kids are very active but are they productive?

There is a difference between activity and productivity. How productive are your actions at work or actions on your farm? Are we being paid for activity or productivity? Are we paying for activity or productivity? Actions at our work places or in our enterprises should result into productivity /profitability. Guide all actions towards achieving productivity.

The point at which you feel comfortable is the exact point you become complacent. The major reason why we do not develop to our full potential is because we become comfortable so fast. We set ourselves small targets and once we achieve them, we feel satisfied.

Ever wondered why some people work till they die? Nothing is as pitiable as seeing an old man/woman toiling for survival. One never stops wondering whether these elderly working people do not have children to take care of them. They clearly did not prepare adequately for their future and are most probably being let down as well by their irresponsible children.

Do you still remember those shopkeepers who used to give you sweets when you were young?

How many of them have moved on or even expanded their businesses? What about the teachers that taught us in primary school?

What do they have to show for all these years of their adult life? All or most of us know that tailor who has never left his location since our childhood. These are no different from most small businesses. Small businesses seem contented with their smallness. Most of these businesses are set up to cater for family needs and once this is achieved, the owners never bother to set higher targets.

Any business you start should serve more than satisfying your family needs. The ultimate goal of starting a business must be to grow as services are offered to customers. When you become a big player in your area, search for other areas in which to expand your business. It is not a crime to operate in places different from your birth or workplaces. Your small business must give birth to other businesses. A living thing gives birth to other living things. A business is a living thing because it grows and (can) die. Growing your business should be your prime goal of being in business. Where do you want to be in two, five, ten, twenty years to come in terms of your business size and strength?

What forces us out of our comfort zones?

It has been said that the hungrier one becomes, the clearer one's mind works and the more sensitive one becomes to the aroma of food. Once one is against the wall, the mind will work overtime to find a way forward.

Several options will be considered and a concerted effort made through trial and error to determine which option works.Some people have moved out of their comfort zones because they no longer find what they are doing as challenging as before.

They want to build something new and see it grow. Most, however, have been forced out of their comfort zones by circumstances. The former option gives one time to prepare themselves as opposed to the latter. When you are forced out of your comfort zone, you have to figure out what to do. Most times it is not easy because we have not been prepared to take care of unfamiliar territory. It is like throwing you into a football match for which you have not trained.

Do not be pushed before you are ready. When you are hired for a job, keep in mind that one day you will have to leave. Never be content with your current stage in life. You are meant to keep moving forward and therefore you must have a plan for your progress from where you are to where you want to be.

WHO ARE YOU PASSING ON THE RESPONSIBILITY TO?

Be deliberate about the character of people you hire.

What is your purpose in the enterprise you are in? There are two major questions employers want answered before they take on or retain staff:
•Will your presence improve their sales or profit levels?
•Is your behaviour helpful for the enterprise to realize improved sales and profits?
The first question requires answers about your skills, experience and past performance.

The second requires answers about your personality. How do you handle easy and difficult customers, colleagues, supervisors and employers? Do you strive to produce the required quality and quantity within set deadlines? Are you the careless type that will cause the enterprise more losses than profits? Are you a perpetual late comer or absentee? How committed are you to your work?

Are you the type that reports to work and does everything else apart from the work you were hired to do? How organized are you and your workplace? Do you easily respect people around you? Do you insist on being paid for everything you do at the work place?

These might be very many questions but believe me any serious employer will want someone who does not hurt their interests. They have hired and possibly fired several people before you and will always look out for those behaviours that have made profits for them or became a work nightmare for them.

     SMALL BUSINESS IS BIG BUSINESS

Give your business ample time to grow. I have seen people close business just after the end of their first rent instalment and I feel bad for them.

A baby is born after nine months, different crops and animals take different number of months to grow to maturity. What does this tell you?

You must be patient and feed your business like a responsible parent does to a baby. A responsible parent follows doctors' orders pertaining to feeding and upbringing of a baby and will always look out for what is best for the baby. Your business is your baby so take care of it like one. No parent worth their name neglects a baby because of some hiccups along the way. When you decide to be in business, have a well thought out plan and mobilize adequate resources with a long term vision in mind.

Moving from one location to another or from one business to another after a short time means that you lack a clear focus on what needs to be done in your business. Just because others are doing the business or just because a rentable space is available does not necessarily mean you can occupy it and transact business. It takes much more than that.

Be that person who is always thinking of better ways of doing whatever you have been assigned. Have an unwavering push for excellence every day. Improve your capacity and capability daily. Be someone whose goals are subordinated to the business. Pursuing your goals should never substitute the push for achieving the goals of the business. Design goals that are in line with the goals of the business so that you grow together.

Our presence within the community must be felt and should matter. We must be a point of reference in whatever we do. We must become benchmarks for extraordinary service.

Understand that all goals are achieved by working as a team. Be a team player who helps others to achieve the overall goal of the business. Help weaker members of your team and coordinate whatever you do with others to create synergies at work. Be proactive at work and find solutions for any challenge. Rather than passing over challenges to others for solutions, be active in finding solutions. Be among the people who never give up till a challenge is overcome.

Become an asset to the business you are in by adding value to it. Search for new opportunities and customers for the business. Take good care of the customers of your business so that they are enticed to buy more of what you are selling. Develop values that are in line with the business virtues being promoted. Every business has core values it stands by. These normally guide their actions and operations.

Motivate the people you work with. Be a cheerleader in all that is done in pursuit of the enterprise's goals. Although several reasons bring employees to the workstation, someone to inspire them to do better every day is very essential for increased performance. We go through a lot of pressures and challenges both at the workplace and in our family settings that mood swings cannot be avoided. Find out what others are going through and help where you can. Helping them find solutions actually eases the burden on them and they are able to focus on working with the team to achieve the set goals.

    SMALL BUSINESS IS BIG BUSINESS

WHAT LEGACY DO YOU WANT TO LEAVE BEHIND?

We are known for what we do but also for what we fail to do. What will your story be?

What do you want to be remembered for?

Wherever you are, wherever you go and whatever you do, people will remember you for either something you did or failed to do in life. Whatever you do, ensure that even long after you have left or are no more, the memories of you are more positive than negative.

We are totally in charge of what the world will remember us for. Build a profile of the person you want to be remembered for. Choose activities or actions which come naturally to you to have an impact on people you live with, in your environment (community, home, work, school etc.) and everyone who looks up to you. Our competence and behaviour shall always be examined by those we work with and for. Be remembered more for your competence and helpful behaviour.

Be remembered for starting and accelerating several projects during your time in action rather than being a disruption at inception and during implementation.

What is it you are doing to impact your community?

When we start businesses, our intention should be more than earning an income through providing required goods and services. We must be deliberate in serving our communities with a purpose of causing a desired change.

Our presence within the community must be felt and should matter. We must be a point of reference in whatever we do. We must become benchmarks for extraordinary service.

Be known for something unique to you only. Even when many people are doing a similar business, choose to stand out by your way of operation and the quality you present to the customers.
Every place and business has people whose opinions you cannot avoid seeking because they have a niche for themselves in that business. You cannot talk about certain businesses and places without specific names coming up. Work harder but more importantly be smarter in your work so that you will be among such people that matter in the community

DO YOU WANT A SMOOTH HAND OVER OR NOT?
Succession planning is a prerequisite for continuity of best practices.

What type of farm will you bequeath to your offspring? How are you using the idle family land? As we grow up, we find ourselves with access to large acreage of family land. Some of us actively participate in development activities on the land whereas others do not.

It is important for us to lay strategies for utilizing available family land or purchasing ours to establish upcountry farms onto which we shall retire after our active working years. Time and again, we get clients who come to us in their later years seeking guidance to invest in enterprises on their individual or family owned land.

Whereas there is no problem with anyone seeking help on how to invest, starting investments in the later years comes with increased risks.

There is less room for making mistakes and learning new lessons at later years in life. Should your investment fail or falter for any one reason, the shock might be unbearable and irreversible. Plan and roll out investments in your earlier years of active service. Starting earlier on in life gives you ample time to manoeuvre around challenges of investing and managing investments. Work as you focus on taking care of your later years of life. These are years when we lack enough energy to do what we feel like and therefore have to rely on others.

Make the best use of available time and opportunities to lay a solid foundation to support you sustainably in your old age. Focus on the time you will lack the energy to actively work.

When is the right time to hand over the reins?

Handing over control to others is not and has never been an easy decision. Everyone in a position of power and influence faces a challenge of who to hand over to and when to hand over especially if they did not plan for it. We must however realize that a time comes when we can no longer handle tasks with a vigour we started with. Losing the power to influence the flow of events scares most people. If the wrong person takes over the decision making position, all previous gains might go to waste. Nothing frustrates like seeing a decision maker messing up a formerly effective and efficient system. Should that person have a vision different from yours, what you started will be turned into a totally different direction.

We have witnessed several politicians taking over reins of power with the support of their god fathers only to turn around and persecute them. Children have abused chances to manage and multiply what their parents pass on to them while still alive. After bungling up these opportunities, these children become a security threat to the parents and other siblings as they are not ashamed to demand for more.

We have grown up seeing parents aging and not giving up their control over anything they sweated for to any of their children till death. They fear that the children might run down what they sweated for all their lives. They cannot stand seeing everything going down the drain under their watch and would prefer that the children mess up when they are gone.

Some have gone ahead to make it known that what the children see and enjoy belongs to them and the children are expected to start their own. The children are informed that the parents' duty towards them is to educate and take care of them while they study. Once studies are done or when the children refuse to study, they are on their own. The older children are helped by their parents to start their own families and guided to cement their relationships to last. Parents only give them a portion of their wealth to help them stabilize their marriages.

As children grow, the parents get to notice and understand characters specific to them. Most times their role is to guide and ensure the children turn out right. They keep giving children various tasks to help them develop different survival skills. Those who take up the given tasks and do them without being persuaded first will most times be in the good books of their parents. Such children subsequently thrive better in the public and private sectors than the disobedient and inactive ones.

Because it is human nature that we shall all age, it is important to plan for these evening days of our lives. We keep praying for more years and time to complete this or that but the truth is that we cannot go on forever.

Decide at what point(s) in your life to hand over the different responsibilities. Give everyone under you and those who look up to you equal and regular opportunities to sharpen their skills and gain experience.

Identify the strengths and weaknesses of everyone you work with and those you would like to work with. Work with them to take advantage of their strengths and minimise the impact of their weaknesses.

Delegate duties to people according to their strengths and help others develop the strengths you need them to have. Let those under you have a feel of the various tasks but do not leave them unsupervised. Encourage them to consult you whenever necessary and give them positive feedback when they do.

Constant supervision will help both you and the one you are giving tasks to accomplish them with minimal wastage. With time and more exposure, they will perform excellently without your supervision.

Establish and regularly strengthen systems of all operations. Having clear systems of operations enables everyone to understand and fulfil their roles in achieving the overall goal

Orient whoever travels this journey with you as soon as they join you. This enables them to understand your way of operation which might differ from what they are accustomed to.

Have systems that work in synergies, build teams that gel together, define available roles and responsibilities clearly, hire competent and enthusiastic staff, place them in their rightful positions, avail required resources and set up an oversight committee for checks and balances.

Have a transition period where you continuously cede power of decision making to those who have shown the capacity to run the business smoothly. They might stumble but show and keep faith in them. Once the preparatory ground works have been set, you have done your work and can comfortably watch from the side-lines. Your counsel shall always be sought because you prepared people who consult when and if necessary.

WE WOULD LOVE TO REMAIN ACTIVE TILL WE DROP DEAD BUT AT WHAT COST?

The law of diminishing returns finally catches up with us.

As we grow, the energy and resolve tend to be in opposition to each other. It is a situation that is commonly defined thus, "the heart is in it 100% but the body disappoints".

The desire to do much more and leave a larger than life legacy has messed up people's lives to an extent that some are mentioned just in passing. Examples of the once mighty that have been reduced to nothing with time abound worldwide. Imagine what a sad day it was for the all conquering Usain Bolt, a sports icon widely known for his signature celebration, when he was thoroughly beaten in a race that he had monopolized for long .If only he had bowed out more graciously at the top of his game but the urge for one more time was too great for him to resist:-a very familiar desire to many of us.

The strengths and weaknesses inherent in us determine how much we can do. They also determine what we cannot do however much we try. Because there are things we easily do and those we struggle to accomplish, it is only fitting that we gradually give in to the younger generation. The dynamic world we live in demands that we keep our dynamism in top gear. Expecting to solve current problems using methods of yester years is dreaming in broad daylight. Technologies and machinery evolve on a nearly daily basis that success and sustainability requires brains that can keep up with the speed of innovations.

As we work over time, we tend to get tired of the monotony of the work we do. You wake up and can already tell what work you will do throughout the day with precision. Even before noon, you are wondering when the day will come to an end. Instead of the new day coming with a motivation to go and work, you would rather stay behind. The successes you have achieved before no longer arouse your inner satisfaction. The weaknesses within you themselves take a toll on you as you realize there is little you can do to change what you have always failed to do.

Welcome the new breed of young staff still boiling with lots of ideas and willing to try out several of those ideas without fear. They are eager to prove themselves to the world and will go an extra mile to show their value.

Why should we be pushed against our will?

We must delegate more responsibilities as we plan for times when we shall be absent. We must be in charge of how we want to go. The opposite breeds trouble most times. Mentor those you wish to take charge of your responsibilities and give them leeway to exercise their capabilities. Give people equal opportunities to shine. You are safer with equally qualified people around you and able to take on the mantle.

HAVE YOU MENTORED YOUR SUCCESSOR?

The "Do It Yourself" mentality stifles business growth across generations. Pass on that vital information to deserving persons.

How much responsibility do you pass on to those under you or those that depend on you?

When people know you as the "do it myself" kind of person, many hesitate doing anything for you unless you tell them to. This is because they are not sure they can do it the way you do it or whether you will even appreciate anyone doing what you like doing on your own.

Give people under your care space to experiment and learn how things are done. Give them guidance and let them take on different tasks as often as possible. This helps build their confidence and with time you will be comfortable letting them take on more challenging tasks. People fear to delegate duties because of mistakes that might arise. Mistakes can only be minimized if we train and guide those we seek to delegate duties to. As you superintend over employees and different categories of people, mentor them into better beings. Give them space and opportunity to practice, make mistakes and correct them as they gain experience. Passing on responsibilities enables one to build a sustainable business and/or brand and promotes succession planning.

When one is denied responsibility, one is bound to act irresponsibly.

As a mentor, help your employees to identify and translate information, understand problems, identify solutions and implement action plans. Work together with them to set goals and actions they need to achieve. Give employees your time and expertize to support development of their work skills so that they generate more money for your business and keep it sustainable. Adopt an open door policy and your employees will thank you for it.

As a coach, show them how things must be done to achieve the desired results. It is within your interest to orient your employees and keep skilling them regularly. Give them space to practice as much as possible under your watch till they perfect what you want them to do. Be patient as they get used to your way of doing things. Some are slow learners naturally but turn out to be the best and most reliable employees if allowed the opportunity to fit in.

It is through mentoring and coaching that you will be able to identify who to assign more responsibilities. Anyone with integrity, shows a willingness to learn and has an eye for detail should be picked out of the pack and taken through more deliberate targeted management trainings. Employees such as these are the right material for leading the rest towards achieving the overall goals of any business.

Chapter SIX:

CONCLUSION

ARE YOU GOING TO PROCRASTINATE AS USUAL OR ACT NOW?

Choice is the sole reason for differences among people. You are the reason you find yourself where you currently are and will be the reason you will be somewhere else in future.

Reading all the self-help books in this world and attending motivational talks will not change anything in your life unless you acknowledge your inadequacies and work towards eliminating them. This book has been written with an intention of shining a spotlight on the various aspects of our lives and how they affect our progress.

Take this as a diagnosis of what you do or do not do. Be honest and thorough in examining yourself. You are the reason you find yourself where you currently are. You are a decision away from changing the status quo in your life. Decide to be a doer. Let us walk the talk.

The difference between your struggles and those who seem to have overcome them is in the actions taken. The choices you make today have a very big bearing on the direction you will take in life.

Although you might not agree with one or several of the opinions in this book, it cannot be totally useless to your life. Pick out lessons that you feel comfortable applying and go on to cause that necessary positive change in your personal life, career and that of your business.

An action-oriented person does not have to agree with everything. They pick on an idea or ideas and mobilize all necessary resources to implement them. May you be one of those willing and ready to implement their ideas.

Schools were established to open up the mind and impart skills to survive and thrive in this dynamic and highly competitive world.

    SMALL BUSINESS IS BIG BUSINESS

Even when we go through such schools, the most important school is one that teaches one how to sell value for profit/ gain. It is one school that puts us at the same level.
It is up to us to go an extra mile and fully utilize our skills or keep lamenting about the impracticability of every opportunity presented before our eyes.

Stop merely reading to complete books. I implore you to always read and analyse information presented. Highlight sections you find important in the book or better still summarize the books you read into easily digestible points.

Incorporate what you read into your routine operations to become better at what you do. You will not know what works and what does not unless you try it out on your own. We are all on a journey to a better future. Some may cross the road before us but our focus should never be diverted elsewhere. Our speeds might differ but our resolve to succeed must never be stemmed by anyone or anything. We owe it to ourselves to hit our targets in life.

We were created and given a blank cheque as well as a blank page. It is upon us to decide what story to write about our desired and fulfilled lives. It is still up to us to determine what value we add in others' lives. Work upon increasing your value and you will ultimately be paid what you are worth. Open up your mind and try out several things you have never tried out before. What you fear trying out might turn out to be your turning point in life. The world of achievers is awash with people who dare to do and/ or go where others dread.

Everything we do has a profit motive. It is not sustainable to simply live by. As national currencies struggle to maintain value overtime, so must we to our lives. The more skills you acquire, the more opportunities you will be able to utilize.

Make deliberate decisions to become better. Every person you admire was deliberate in their actions and omissions. They chose ventures to invest in and mobilized necessary resources to generate as much money as possible. As the ventures stabilized and became sustainably profitable, they made strides in other areas.

Pursue one venture and nurture it to sustainable growth. Keep innovating regularly and develop multiple income streams that feed into each other. Each of us has a dream. Dreams may be similar but the difference comes in how each one of us understands them and sets out to implement what needs to be done. The ease and speed of realizing a dream depends upon how well you focus on knowing and controlling most parameters in life and business.

Successful people have a master plan of what should be done to the last detail. Do not take anything for granted. Only you can realize your dream because it is clearer in your mind. Are you an asset or a liability to your workplace? Whatever you do either results in value addition or loss of revenue for the enterprise. Your actions at work are largely influenced by your habits. If you always go to work late, you will always lag behind in work assignments; if you are moody it will surely show at your workplace.

Work extra hard on your weaknesses and ensure you are more of an asset than a liability at your workplace.

Meetings should not be held to discipline you but rather to discuss how best they can take care of your requirements. Help companies/enterprises benefit from your presence on their payroll.

Describing small business by number of employees and size of working space is becoming extinct due to focus on efficiency and effectiveness. Due to limited land and unreliable labour force, intensive and mechanized operations are increasingly being taken on to improve output from small areas of work.

There is no more excuse not to work smart. Small land should never be used as an excuse not to ensure surplus returns for any inputs. Automate and add value to increase good quality output that can be sold at higher prices for longer periods in varied geographical locations.

Start with what is available and accessible to you. Muster whatever resources you can and put in your personal time and effort to nurture this new venture like parents nurture their babies. Ten years from now, you should not be looking back in regret. You should be happy with your results. Commit to deliberate planning, mobilizing, organizing, coordinating, leading and controlling processes.

Planning deals with coming up with all activities that determine the future or course of action for any enterprise; mobilizing involves getting together all necessary resources; organizing is a process of turning plans into action through division of labour and delegation of authority; coordinating promotes synergy of actions and work; leading is influencing others to achieve set goals through a number of interpersonal processes and actions; controlling focuses on ensuring that performance conforms to plans.

GO ON AND DO SOMETHING YOU HAVE NOT DONE BEFORE.

 SMALL BUSINESS IS BIG BUSINESS

BUSINESS IDEAS, REFERENCES AND RESOURCES BUSINESS IDEAS

These ideas were thought of by people like you. Exercise your mind more and come up with ideas you can work upon uniquely.

The following are businesses to start with Uganda shillings thirty thousand (30,000) to Uganda shillings one hundred fifty thousand (150,000) in Uganda.
1. Selling Vegetables
2. Hawking anything used by human beings.
3. Selling Mivumba/second hand clothes
4. Washing bay business in small towns
5. Shoe shining business
6. Photography
7. Rearing local breed chicken
8. Mobile manicure and pedicure
9. Chapati/pancakes and other fried breakfast eats
10. Roasted ground nuts/soya/popcorn/sim-sim

Businesses to start with Uganda shillings three hundred thousand (300,000) to Uganda shillings three million (3,000,000)
1. Kinyozi/Barber shop
2. Salon
3. Grocery
4. Boutique in small towns
5. Selling women handbags
6. Selling women clothes/children clothes/men shirts
7. Farming tomatoes, onions, pineapple, watermelon, maize and beans.
8. Photocopy, scanning and printing business
9. Investing in shares and bonds

10. Processing all agricultural products into soft drinks/ honey/meat products/fish/milk

Businesses to start with Uganda shillings five million (5,000,000) to Uganda shillings fifteen million (15,000,000).
1. Fast Food Restaurant
2. A small pub
3. First star Hotel
4. Classic Barber Shop
5. Salon/dry cleaning services in posh estates
6. General shop or groceries
7. Laundry contract business
8. Classic Car Wash
9. Starting Mobile money Shop
10. Starting banking agency business
11. Starting motor cycle spare parts business
12. Starting a cosmetics shop
13. Starting an Audit firm
14.Starting a consulting firm

Businesses to start with Uganda shillings fifteen million (15,000,000) to Uganda shillings thirty million (30,000,000).
1. Electronic shop business
2. A pub in major cities
3. A restaurant in Central Business District
4. Fast Food restaurant in Central Business District
5. A jewellery shop
6. Furniture making business
7. Large scale farming or tree growing and sale after 5years
8. A school or rental housing units
9. A SACCO or buying land for sale to other people at higher price after 1 year

10. Starting wines and spirits wholesale shop
11. Starting a bookshop
12. Starting a taxi business
13. Starting a motor vehicle spare parts business
14. Starting a chemist shop
15. Starting a security firm
16. Starting a recording studio

Businesses to start in Uganda with over Uganda shillings three hundred million (300,000,000)
1. Building large scale rental houses
2. Real Estate firm
3. Business of supplying services of earth movers
4. Subcontractors/applying for tenders in any business
5.Research into future products and needs

The above information has been widely shared over face book and WhatsApp where I got it. The author is unknown. Your own personal research into actual costs of starting the above mentioned businesses is highly advised. Use the information as a guide.

Purchasers of this book from outside Uganda are advised to convert the above start-up capital into their local currencies.

101 Best Side Business Ideas to Start While Working Full-Time (Ryan Robinson)
1. Graphic Design.
2. Web Design.
3. Web Development.
4. Tax Preparation.

     SMALL BUSINESS IS BIG BUSINESS

5. Commission-Only Sales.

6. Online courses.

7. eBooks.

8. Instagram Marketing.

9. Online coaching.

10. Podcasting.

11. Amazon Reselling.

12. Local Business Consulting.

13. Phone Case Business.

14. Affiliate Sales and Marketing.

15. Virtual Assistant.

16. Remote English Teacher/Tutor.

17. SAT Tutor/High School Private Tutor.

18. Social Media Manager.

19. Google Paid Ad Specialist.

20. Start a Blog.

21. Presentation Design Consultant.

22. Travel Consultant.

23. Landing Page Specialist.

24. Interior Design Consultant.

25. Housesitter.

26. Babysitter.

27. Property Manager.

28. Sell on Etsy.

29. Ebay Sales.

30. Fiverr Gigs

31. College Admission Essay Editor.

32. Portrait Photographer.

33. Wedding Photographer.

34. Online Dating Consultant.

35. Writing Erotic Fiction.

36. Writing Greeting Cards.

37. WordPress Website Consultant.
38. Drive for Uber or Lyft.
39. Rent Your Car on Turo.
40. Art Collector.
41. Catering Business.
42. Develop an App.
43. Online News Correspondent.
44. Patent Something.
45. Buy and Sell Domain Names.
46. Start a Popup Shop.
47. Brew Your own Beer.
48. Freelance Proofreading and Editing.
49. Buy Used Electronics and Refurbish Them.
50. Data Analysis.
51. Acquire Parts from Electronics Store.
52. Copywriting for Websites.
53. Licensed Product Distributor.
54. Fill Out Online Surveys.
55. Airbnb Host.
56. Personal Fitness Trainer.
57. Yoga or Meditation Instructor.
58. Start a You Tube Channel.
59. Translator.
60. Tour Guide.
61. Music Instructor.
62. Stock Photographer.
63. Ghostwriter.
64. Online Subcontracting.
65. DJ-ing.
66. Clothing Alterations and Tailoring.
67. Teach DIYs

68. Baking.
69. Being a Task Rabbit.
70. Freelance Content Marketing.
71. Freelance Ebook Writing.
72. Investing Your Money.
73. Investing Others' Money.
74. Accounting and Bookkeeping.
75. Building a Niche Website.
76. Car Washing and Detailing.
77. Caregiving.
78. Carpet Cleaning.
79. House Cleaning.
80. Child Care.
81. Computer Repair.
82. Modelling.
83. Computer Training and Lessons.
84. Contract Customer Service.
85. Dog Walking.
86. Real Estate Sale Consultant.
87. Making Custom Furniture.
88. Making Handmade Jewellery
89. Being a Gig walker.
90. Home Appraisal.
91. Human Billboard.
92. Purchasing an Existing Website.
93. Mobile Laundry Service.
94. Junk Removal Service.
95. Becoming a Notary Public.
96. Wedding Planning.
97. Event and Party Planning.
98. Becoming a Personal Chef.

99. Pet Sitting.
100. Pet grooming.
101. Pool Cleaning.
102. Private Labelling and Selling Products on Amazon.
103. Officiating Recreational Sports Games.
104. Selling on Tee Spring.
105. Build Custom Software for Freelance Clients.
106. Coaching Sports Teams.
107. T-Shirt Printing Business.
108. Vehicle Advertising.
109. Window Cleaning Services.
110. Working on Mechanical Turk.
111. Yard Work Services.
112. Public Speaking.
113. College Counselling.
114. Making Seasonal Decorations.
115. Snowploughing.
116. Selling Handmade Clothing and Garments.
117. Antique Instructor.
118. Dance Instructor.
119. Part-time Bicycle Delivery.
120. Home-Based Makeup Services.
121. Voice-Over Talent.
122. Buying and Selling Cars.
123. Small Business Marketing Consultant.
124. Professional Organising.
125. Rent out your space.
126. Build a Chrome Extension.
127. Floral Design.
128. Recycling.

     SMALL BUSINESS IS BIG BUSINESS

100 HOME BUSINESS IDEAS (Copied from a WhatsApp group)

1.   Proposal Writing.
2.   Real Estate Agency.
3.   Information Marketing.
4.   Blogging.
5.   Web Publishing.
6.   Selling Fruits.
7.   Baking Confectioneries.
8.   Selling Honey.
9.   Home Tutoring.
10.   Freelance Marketing.
11.   Freelance Writing.
12.   E-books Publishing.
13.   Affiliate Marketing.
14.   Crafts Business.
15.   Bread Making.
16.   Weight Loss Classes.
17.   Exercise Instructor.
18.   Party Planner.
19.   Business Plan Writing.
20.   Business Broker.
21.   Aerobics Classes.
22.   Carpet Cleaning.
23.   Corporate Cleaning Services.
24.   Computer Instructor.
25.   Dance Instructor.
26.   Graphic Designer.
27.   Web Designer.
28.   Computer Programmer.
29.   Computer Repairs.
30.   Mobile Phone Repairs.

31.   Charging of Car and Phone Batteries.
32.   Time Management Consultant.
33.   Cooking Services.
34.   Cosmetics Sales.
35.   Dating Services.
36.   Directory Publisher.
37.   Editor.
38.   Email Marketing.
39.   Employment Agency.
40.   Event Management.
41.   Event Planner.
42.   Errand Services.
43.   Export Agent.
44.   Ezine Publishing.
45.   Facialist.
46.   Hair Stylist.
47.   Beautician.
48.   Make-up Artistry.
49.   Freelance Photographer.
50.   Ghost Writer.
51.   Greetings Card Designer.
52.   Food Delivery Services.
53.   Homemade Story Books.
54.   You Tube Videos.
55.   Information Broker.
56.   Infopreneur.
57.   Internet Marketing.
58.   Internet Service Provider.
59.   Internet Recruiting.
60.   Interpreter/Translator.

61.   Foreign Language Teacher.
62.   Mailing List Service.
63.   Market Research.
64.   Monogramming.
65.   Music Lessons.
66.   Nanny Services.
67.   Online Internet Training.
68.   Painting.
69.   Payroll Services.
70.   Martial Arts Instructor.
71.   Pet Training.
72.   Selling Pet Products.
73.   Proofreader.
74.   Public Relations Agency.
75.   Public/Motivational Speaker.
76.   Reporter.
77.   CV/Resume Writing Services.
78.   Self-Improvement Seminars.
79.   Self-Publishing.
80.   Song Writing.
81.   Teaching.
82.   Technical Writer.
83.   Telephone Answering Services.
84.   Tour Guide.
85.   Travel Agency.
86.   Scholarship and Overseas study Consultant.
87.   Typing Services.
88.   Mobile Supermarket.
89.   Writing Press Releases.
90.   SMS Marketing.
94.   Viewing Centre.
95.   Daycare Centre.

91.   Excursion Services.
92.   Holiday Camp.
93.   Video game Centre.
96.   Car Wash service.
97.   Selling chilled Drinks.
98.   Yoghurt.
99.   Home Business Centre.
100.   School Dropping and Picking services.

REFERENCES AND RESOURCES

500 BUSINESS IDEAS(A May 2010 Uganda Investment Authority FINAL REPORT for Generation and Up-dating of Business Ideas by Business Synergies Public and Private Management Consultants)

THE 100 PRACTICAL WAYS TO EMPOWER YOURSELF (SKILLS EMPOWERMENT AFRICA)
A skills empowerment E-book compiled by Andrew Otai
https:/www.facebook.com/skillsempoermentafrica

200 PROFITABLE BUSINESS IDEAS IN KENYA (A 2017 BOOK BY TITUS MIRIERI).

BUSINESS IDEAS WORTH YOUR ATTENTION (A BOOK BY NICHOLAS KATUSHABE)

Remember to invite Jimmy Muhinda as soon as possible to share the book and inspire you and your team at your next event. Allow him to join your development process.
Telephone/WhatsApp: +256 772 563048
+256 702 662840
E-mail: jmhnda@yahoo.com

9 789997 099330 7